Your Happy Healthy Pet™

Guinea Pig

2nd Edition

Audrey Pavia

This book is printed on acid-free paper.♾

Howell Book House
Published by Wiley Publishing, Inc., Hoboken, New Jersey

For general information on our other products and services or to obtain technical support please contact our Customer Care Department within the U.S. at (800) 762-2974, outside the U.S. at (317) 572-3993 or fax (317) 572-4002.

Wiley also publishes its books in a variety of electronic formats. Some content that appears in print may not be available in electronic books. For more information about Wiley products, please visit our Web site at www.wiley.com.

Library of Congress Cataloging-in-Publication Data:
Pavia, Audrey.
Guinea pig / Audrey Pavia—2nd ed.
p. cm.— (Your happy healthy pet)
Includes index.
ISBN-13: 978-1-63026-012-5 (paperback)
1. Guinea pigs as pets. I. Title. II. Series.
SF459.G9P38 2005
636.935'92—dc22
2005002070

Printed in the United States of America

Second Edition

Book design by Melissa Auciello-Brogan
Cover design by Michael J. Freeland
Book production by Wiley Publishing, Inc. Composition Services

Acknowledgments

Special thanks to Tracy Iverson with the Oregon Cavy Breeders Society.

About the Author

Audrey Pavia is an award-winning freelance writer who specializes in animal subjects. She has written sixteen books and hundreds of articles about animals. Audrey is a frequent contributor to *Critters USA* magazine, a former 4-H project member, and shares her home in California with a variety of pets.

About Howell Book House

Since 1961, Howell Book House has been America's premier publisher of pet books. We're dedicated to companion animals and the people who love them, and our books reflect that commitment. Our stable of authors—training experts, veterinarians, breeders, and other authorities—is second to none. And we've won more Maxwell Awards from the Dog Writers Association of America than any other publisher.

As we head toward the half-century mark, we're more committed than ever to providing new and innovative books, along with the classics our readers have grown to love. This year, we're launching several exciting new initiatives, including redesigning the Howell Book House logo and revamping our biggest pet series, Your Happy Healthy Pet, with bold new covers and updated content. From bringing home a new puppy to competing in advanced equestrian events, Howell has the titles that keep animal lovers coming back again and again.

Contents

Shopping List

You'll need to do a bit of stocking up before you bring your new guinea pig home. Below is a basic list of some must-have supplies. For more detailed information on the selection of each item, consult chapter 5.

- ☐ Cage or hutch
- ☐ Nest box
- ☐ Food bowl
- ☐ Water bottle with metal tip
- ☐ Hay rack
- ☐ Guinea pig food
- ☐ Bedding
- ☐ Chewing blocks
- ☐ Pet carrier
- ☐ Brush and comb
- ☐ Toys
- ☐ Nail trimmer
- ☐ Hay

There are likely to be a few other items that you're dying to pick up before bringing your guinea pig home. Use the following blanks to note any additional items you'll be shopping for.

- ☐ ______________________
- ☐ ______________________
- ☐ ______________________
- ☐ ______________________
- ☐ ______________________
- ☐ ______________________
- ☐ ______________________
- ☐ ______________________
- ☐ ______________________
- ☐ ______________________
- ☐ ______________________

Pet Sitter's Guide

We can be reached at (__)_____-_______ Cellphone (__)_____-_______

____

We will return on ____________ (date) at ____________ (approximate time)

Guinea Pig's Name ______________________________

Breed, Age, and Sex ______________________________

Important Names and Numbers

Vet's Name ______________________ Phone (__) _____-_______

Address ____________________________________

Emergency Vet's Name __________________ Phone (__) ____-_______

Address ____________________________________

Poison Control ____________________________ (or call vet first)

Other individual to contact in case of emergency __________________

____

Care Instructions

In the following blanks, let the sitter know what to feed, how much, and when; when to offer out-of-cage time; when to give treats; and explain cage cleaning requirements.

Morning____________________________________

____

Evening ____________________________________

____

Any special medical needs __________________________

____

Grooming instructions____________________________

____

My guinea pig's favorite playtime activities, quirks, and other tips __________

____

____

____

____

____

Part I
The World of the Guinea Pig

The Guinea Pig

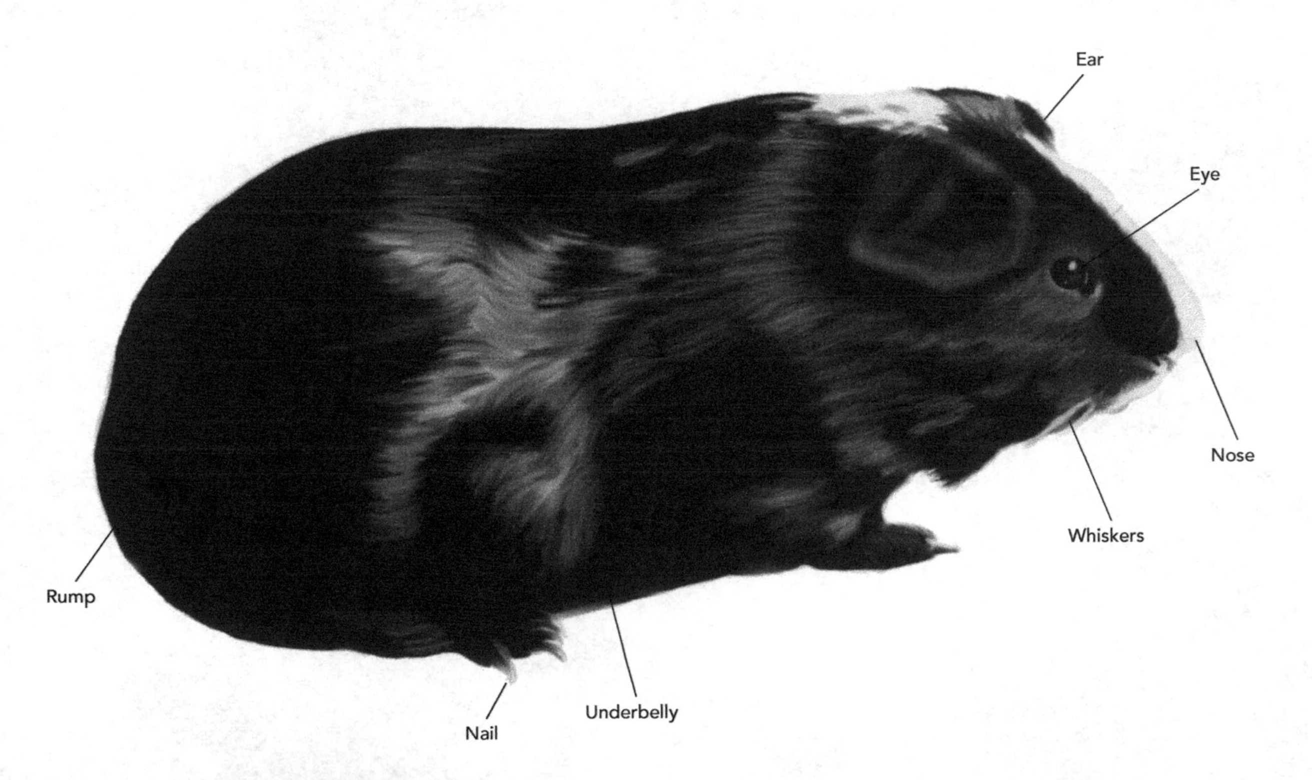

Chapter 1

Guinea Pigs as Pets

People who live with guinea pigs know that dogs and cats have not cornered the market when it comes to love and affection. Guinea pigs can be very warm-hearted creatures. They adore being petted and love to fall asleep in the lap of a person they trust. Guinea pigs have a large capacity for affection and thrive when they receive love in return.

Guinea pigs are not always thought of as intelligent creatures, but in reality, they are a lot smarter than most people think. They are bright animals with complex social structures who develop relationships with individual people and even animals of other species.

In the wild, guinea pigs are food for predators, and this makes them suspicious by nature. How else would they survive? Because of this, they are often fearful and nervous. But once they learn that they are safe in their environment, the depth of their personality comes shining through.

In the world of pet ownership, there are few things more rewarding than knowing that a guinea pig loves you and trusts you. This trust is something you must earn. You can only establish this kind of rapport with your pet once you have spent time with him, showing him that you are worthy of his confidence.

Life with a guinea pig means staying on your toes. They are active and inquisitive and are always exploring their environment. Aside from being endearing, this kind of behavior can also get them into trouble. That's why guinea pig owners need to be especially vigilant about their pets' whereabouts at all times.

Many people find it surprising to know that guinea pigs can learn to recognize the sound of their favorite humans' voices. They can also learn that the opening of the refrigerator means a treat and the crackling of a plastic bag means

The Advantages of Guinea Pigs

More and more people are discovering what makes guinea pigs such wonderful pets. Some of the things people like most about guinea pigs are:

- They don't need long walks or bathroom breaks.
- They don't need a lot of room.
- They can be trained to use a litter box.
- They are entertaining and curious animals.
- They are social and can bond with their owners and other animals.

food is on its way. Many guinea pigs can also be trained to do a variety of simple tricks. Some talented guinea pigs can learn to use a litter box.

Like all animals, guinea pigs have body language that they use to communicate with members of their own species. Humans who learn to comprehend that language will better understand what their guinea pigs are telling them. Once there is this kind of understanding between human and guinea pig, the bond deepens.

The Right Pet for You?

Compared to a dog, a guinea pig is a fairly easy pet to own. Guinea pigs don't need to go on long walks every day or be taken to obedience school. The owner of a guinea pig can leave their pet alone for several hours a day and not have to worry about the animal needing bathroom breaks.

On the other hand, guinea pigs are not maintenance-free pets. They are social creatures who need a lot of love and attention, along with quality care.

To determine whether a guinea pig would be a good pet for you, think about your lifestyle. Will your job, school, or other commitments allow you to set aside time every day to spend with your guinea pig? Guinea pigs need daily interaction to meet their emotional needs. If you must leave a guinea pig alone for many hours each day, you should probably have two guinea pigs so they can keep each other company. Are you willing to make the commitment to spend several hours a day with your guinea pig and possibly to take on the responsibility of owning two of them?

Guinea pigs also need daily exercise. Your guinea pig will be confined to a cage or hutch most of the time. Will you be able to let him out each day for supervised activity?

You'll need to scrub your guinea pig's cage every week or so and clean out the soiled areas every day. You'll also have to feed your pet on a regular schedule and make sure he has fresh, clean water all the time. Can you work these tasks into your schedule?

Think about where you live. Do you have room to house a guinea pig? Keep in mind that a guinea pig needs a spacious cage that will keep him safe from other pets and predators and plenty of room to romp during supervised play times.

You must be willing to make changes in your environment. Guinea pigs are chewers, and homes that have guinea pigs must be chew proofed. This requires considerable time and effort. And then there's always the chance that your guinea pig may outwit you and damage something valuable with those destructive teeth. Are you willing to face this possibility?

Guinea pigs are very social creatures and will be terribly lonely and bored if you do not spend time with them every day.

Guinea pigs are curious and entertaining—and adorable.

If you or someone in your family has allergies, will you be able to live with a guinea pig? Guinea pigs can cause severe allergic reactions in some people. Take everyone in your family to a pet store or guinea pig breeder to see if anyone has allergies to guinea pig dander. Find this out *before* you bring a guinea pig home.

If you love other animals as well, then you probably have another issue to think about—other pets. Do you have a dog or a cat? If you add a guinea pig to your home, you will need to think about how your other pets will act toward the newcomer and how the inclusion of the guinea pig is going to affect their lives.

Guinea pigs are instinctively afraid of dogs, and rightfully so, since a dog can easily kill a guinea pig. Most dogs are aggressive toward rodents and will attack them. Cats, while not very dangerous to a rodent as large as an adult guinea pig, can also be less than friendly to guinea pigs. You will need to do a lot of work to either keep your guinea pig separated from your other animals or somehow ensure that they all get along (remembering that this is not always possible).

An important point that many people fail to consider is the legality of guinea pig ownership. Many ordinances do not allow pet rodents in residential areas. Are you zoned for guinea pigs? This, of course, is best discovered before you bring home a new pet.

Another consideration is cost. The price of the guinea pig and his cage is just the beginning. After you bring your pet home, you will have to pay for food, possible spaying or neutering, and vet bills should your guinea pig become ill.

But most important of all, are you willing to make an emotional commitment to your guinea pig? Are you prepared to accept responsibility for a living creature who is solely dependent on you for his well-being? Are you willing to make your pet's health and happiness a priority in your life? If your answer to all these questions is yes, then you might be ready to join the ranks of happy guinea pig owners everywhere.

Guinea Pigs and Children

Children and guinea pigs can be great friends. But you need to ask yourself if your kids are old enough to learn how to handle the guinea pig properly and treat him with respect. These are small animals, and they can easily be hurt. Very young children cannot be expected to understand that a guinea pig needs to be held a certain way and that a guinea pig should not be picked up without adult supervision.

While cavies have traditionally been thought of as a child's pet, a child should never have the sole responsibility for taking care of a guinea pig.

Responsible older children will even be able to take a large role in caring for a guinea pig. But you will still have to take responsibility for the pet, no matter what your children promised when you got him. Even though they have the best of intentions, most children do not have the attention span required for the care of a guinea pig, who may live as long as seven years.

Although a parent should never expect a child to take full responsibility for any pet, allotting guinea pig chores is one way to let everyone in the family participate in the pet's life. Set reasonable goals for your child, depending on their maturity. A younger child may help out by offering the guinea pig a treat (such as fruit or green vegetables) every day, while an older child can be expected to feed the guinea pig and check his water supply daily.

Just watching your guinea pig can be a lot of fun.

Whatever your child's responsibility, praise him or her for a job well done. You don't want to make the guinea pig a subject your child would rather avoid. And remember that you must always be there to monitor the pet's well-being. No child should be given unsupervised responsibility for any animal. Children cannot be expected to recognize signs of illness in a guinea pig or to be able to judge the guinea pig's well-being. An adult should always be the pet's primary caregiver, ready to take over the child's responsibilities if they forget them. Otherwise, it is the helpless guinea pig who suffers in your struggle to teach your child responsibility.

TIP

Your Children's Friends

Although your child may be mature enough to handle the guinea pig carefully and gently, you cannot be sure their friends will be. If your child wants to show off the pet to friends, make sure you are there to supervise the show and tell.

In addition to helping care for the guinea pig, children can have fun with these pets. Your child can make toys for the guinea pig out of toilet paper tubes, paper bags, empty tissue boxes, and other safe objects. Let your child use their imagination.

Another fun guinea pig activity is simple observation. This is a good way to have your child learn about animal behavior in general and rodent behavior in particular. Another good way to get your child involved with their pet is to join a 4-H program. See chapter 10 for more information on this hobby.

Younger children can also have a great deal of fun with a guinea pig, although they will need to be supervised. A guinea pig is a great way to teach them to respect other living things. Show them how to be gentle with their pet guinea pig. Let them pet the guinea pig on the floor, but don't allow them to pick him up. Young children can get startled or impatient, or might just not be able to hold the guinea pig properly. As a result, the guinea pig might get dropped and injured. Instead, hold the guinea pig yourself and allow your child to pet him.

Chapter 2

A Guinea Pig History

The sweet, simple little animal we know as the guinea pig has a rich and exotic past. Her history begins with the earliest rodent fossils from the Paleocene Era, around 57 million years ago. Different rodent families evolved from these very early mammals until, 20 million years ago, during the mid-Miocene Era, the *Caviidae* family of rodents appeared in South America. From these ancient species, the modern guinea pig evolved.

The guinea pig belongs to the *cavia* genus, of which there are four other members, all wild cavies still living in South America. The domestic guinea pig has been living with humans for thousands of years and is similar to—but not exactly the same as—her wild cousins. These wild relatives are found in the grasslands and scrub of South America, as well as in desert climates and the high altitudes of the Andes Mountains. The scientific name for the domestic guinea pig—or cavy, as she is also known—is *Caviidae porcellus.*

The guinea pig is a rodent and is related to such diverse creatures as the mouse, beaver, porcupine, and capybara. Like most rodents, the guinea pig is an herbivore, or plant eater. Her front teeth, or incisors, grow continuously, as do the incisors of all rodents, and must be worn down through gnawing.

Most guinea pigs—domestic and wild—share the same physical form. They have a round, cobby body and a large head that makes up about one-third of the animal's length. The eyes and ears are big. The hind feet have three clawed toes, while the front feet have four toes with claws. The guinea pig has no tail.

Both wild and domestic guinea pigs are known for their ability to reproduce quickly. Females are capable of bearing young at 1 month old. Gestation takes nearly two to three months in guinea pigs, depending on the species. Litters usually consist of three or four pups.

Wild guinea pigs live in social groups and communicate using squeals, squeaks, and squawks.

The wild cavy cousins of the domestic guinea pig live in social groups called herds, in which they use a series of squeals, squeaks, and squawks to communicate with one another. To keep peace within the herd, cavies establish an order of dominance. A male cavy becomes the dominant animal in the group and is the only one allowed to mate with the females.

Because wild cavies have few physical defenses against predators, they use their social groupings for protection. Members of a wild herd create trails between their burrows so they can easily run for cover when danger approaches. They also warn one another of lurking predators with vocalizations and body language that other cavies can understand.

Domesticating Guinea Pigs

Thousands of years ago, the native peoples of South America ate wild cavies. The Incas eventually domesticated the animal around 5000 B.C.E. They used cavies for food and in religious ceremonies. The Spaniards who arrived in Peru in the sixteenth century had never before seen these animals.

What's in a Name?

Different theories abound as to how the cavy came to be called the guinea pig, when she is not a pig at all. Some historians speculate that since cavy meat tastes somewhat like pork, people began to refer to the animal as a pig. The term *guinea* may be a mispronunciation of Guyana, a Central American country where the animals were acquired by European traders.

Another theory asserts that these small animals were sold by Dutch merchants for one guinea, an old coin. Because people thought the little animals resembled pigs, they became guinea pigs.

After the Spanish conquest of the Inca Empire in the mid-1500s, Dutch merchants brought cavies back to Europe. They became popular as pets among aristocrats in Europe during the 1600s, in large part because Queen Elizabeth I of England kept one as a pet.

Over the next three hundred years, Europeans began deliberately breeding guinea pigs for different traits. In the nineteenth century, British immigrants brought some of these specially bred guinea pigs to America, and the cavy fancy in the United States was set to flourish.

Guinea Pigs in the United States

In the United States, specialized breeding of guinea pigs for exhibition began in the early 1900s. In 1910, the National Pet Stock Association was formed to govern the breeding of small mammals such as rabbits, guinea pigs, and hamsters. In 1923, the organization changed its name to the American Rabbit and Cavy Breeders Association, and it dealt only with rabbits and guinea pigs.

Cavy breeders opted to leave the American Rabbit and Cavy Breeders Association in 1952 and formed their own organization, the American Cavy Breeders Association (ACBA). The American Rabbit and Cavy Breeders Association became the American Rabbit Breeders Association (ARBA) and began dealing only with rabbits.

Eventually, the American Cavy Breeders Association reunited with the American Rabbit Breeders Association, and now the ACBA functions as a division of the ARBA. To this day, the ARBA is still the governing body for the guinea pig fancy in the United States.

The guinea pig is now a popular pet in the United States because of her affectionate nature and easy care. Guinea pig fanciers breed their animals to exhibit in events around the country. The guinea pig has also thrived as a companion, and millions of children—and adults—have developed relationships with this sweet little creature.

Guinea Pigs Today

Today in the United States, the guinea pig is mainly a beloved pet and companion. In North America and Europe, the guinea pig's main function is as a pet, show, and research animal. Specially bred guinea pigs are sold to laboratories, where they are used to study human diseases. Approximately 500,000 guinea pigs are used in scientific research each year. That's why in English we use the word *guinea pig* to mean any creature who is the subject of a scientific experiment.

Guinea pigs today are beloved pets and are also exhibited at guinea pig shows.

In South America, where the guinea pig was domesticated, the animal is still used for food and in religious ceremonies. Known as the *cuy* in South American culture, the guinea pig is eaten by people of all social classes because of the high protein content of her meat. Guinea pig meat is also eaten in some urban areas in North America where Latin American people live.

In small villages in the Andes Mountains, guinea pigs are commonly raised in the home, usually in the kitchen. Here the inhabitants of the home live in close quarters with the animals. In large cities such as Lima, Peru, and La Paz, Bolivia, guinea pigs are also sometimes raised at home. However, commercial breeding of guinea pigs for food is becoming more common.

Famous Guinea Pigs

President Theodore Roosevelt had several pet guinea pigs. Guinea pigs have also played important roles in fiction, including Geraldo (the guinea pig in Stephen King's *The Stand*) and Rodney (a guinea pig with actor Chris Rock's voice in the 1998 film *Dr. Dolittle*).

The guinea pig is an important factor in the economies of several South American countries. Even the guinea pig's manure, a byproduct of the commercial guinea pig meat trade, is used as a fertilizer.

A Link to the Spirits

In South America, the guinea pig is believed to have great powers of healing. In Indian cultures, she is used to diagnose and remove sickness from the bodies of ailing patients. It is also thought that the guinea pig has the power to appease the spirits.

One tradition calls for the animal to be set free in the Ecuadorian Andes. A garment from the sick person is draped over the guinea pig, and pieces of ribbon and yarn are attached to the cloth. It is believed the guinea pig will remove the illness from the person through the clothing and then take the disease to a place where it can do no harm. For the guinea pig to do this, the family of the ill person must take the guinea pig to a sacred place in the Andes called Quinchi Urco, where she is set free to live among the wild cavies that still roam there.

The guinea pig is also used in a number of other rituals in South America. It is believed that the guinea pig can help people pass from one stage of life to another. The animal also plays a large part in the celebration of Patron Saints Day.

Chapter 3

Guinea Pig Diversity

In nature, there's just one type and color of guinea pig. However, over the years breeders have produced many beautiful varieties of guinea pigs from that single wild strain. How did this happen? How did the tremendous variety that now exists develop from one type of guinea pig?

There is a large degree of genetic diversity in every animal that reproduces sexually. This genetic diversity enables a species to adapt to changes in its environment, making the species better able to survive in a shifting world. To put it simply, a guinea pig inherits two genes for a specific trait, coat color for example—one from his father and one from his mother. Each of the genes is either dominant or recessive, and the color of the guinea pig's coat depends on which of the two genes is dominant.

When guinea pigs became domesticated, human beings began to control the animals' breeding. When an unusual trait showed up in a guinea pig, this animal was bred with another guinea pig who had a similar trait. The unusual trait often turned up in the guinea pigs' offspring, rather than being lost again, perhaps forever, as it would have been if the unusual guinea pig had mated with a normal guinea pig on his own. In this way, guinea pig breeders have been able to produce the many beautiful colors and varieties described in this chapter. New and even more amazing varieties are still being developed.

Underneath the fancy coat, though, a purebred guinea pig is the same as any other guinea pig and still needs plenty of affection and care.

Guinea Pig Patterns and Colors

Guinea pigs come in a number of patterns and colors, each with its own unique beauty. Individual colors can be found within each of the following patterns.

- **Agouti pattern**—The hair shaft of an agouti-colored guinea pig has several bands of color. Two or more alternating light or dark bands characterize the agouti pattern. The eyes must be a specific color associated with each individual agouti color. Wild guinea pigs all have the original agouti coloring.
- **Marked pattern**—Guinea pigs with the marked pattern are usually white with patterns of another color throughout their bodies.
- **Self pattern**—This term is used to describe solid-colored guinea pigs who have a uniform color throughout their entire body.
- **Solid pattern**—This is similar to the self pattern, except that it may include agouti and other mixed-color fur as long as this fur does not create a pattern or marking.

Guinea pigs come in a very wide variety of colors and patterns.

While each breed has its own breed standard and color varieties, common colors can be found in many different breeds. Here are some of the most common guinea pig colors and color combinations.

- **Beige**—These guinea pigs are beige all over their bodies, including their ears and feet. Their eyes are pink.
- **Black**—In guinea pigs, black is a deep, rich color that goes all the way to the skin, with matching ears and feet. The eyes are also black.
- **Blue**—Blue can be described as a medium shade of gray with a blue or lavender cast. The eyes of a blue guinea pig are dark blue.
- **Brindle**—Brindle, a combination also commonly seen in dogs, is an intermingling of red and black hairs. The brindle pattern appears consistently all over the body, and the eyes are dark.
- **Broken color**—This is more of a pattern than a color. Broken color guinea pigs have coats with clean-cut patches of two or more recognized colors. Exceptions are the tortoiseshell, Himalayan, tortoiseshell and white, Dalmatian, and Dutch colorations.
- **Chocolate**—The deep, dark brown of a chocolate guinea pig is carried all the way to the skin. The eyes are brown or dark brown with a red cast.
- **Cream**—This is a delicate off-white that is even all over. The eyes of a cream guinea pig are red or dark.
- **Dalmatian**—Just like the dog of the same name, Dalmatian guinea pigs have a coat with dark spots over a white background. The spots can be beige, black, blue, chocolate, cream, lilac, orange, or red.
- **Dutch**—The Dutch-colored guinea pig has dark coloration on the chest, neck, forelegs, and face, in combination with white. The markings are clear and distinct.
- **Golden agouti**—These guinea pigs are a chestnut color with an undercoat of blue-black. The coat should also have black ticking. The eyes are dark.
- **Himalayan**—A Himalayan guinea pig is white with black markings on the nose, feet, and ears. The eyes are pink.
- **Lilac**—This is a medium gray color with a purplish tint that is evenly spread over the guinea pig's entire body, ears, and feet. The eyes are pink or dark with a ruby cast.
- **Red**—Red guinea pigs are a deep, rich red with matching ears and feet. The eyes are dark.

Guinea Pig Vocabulary

Cavy: guinea pig

Boar: male guinea pig

Sow: female guinea pig

- **Red-eyed orange**—As the name implies, these guinea pigs are reddish-orange with ruby red eyes.
- **Roan**—This color combination consists of white hairs mixed with one or two other colors. The eyes and ears match the color of the nonwhite hair.
- **Silver agouti**—Silver agouti is a bright silver-white, which is caused by a blue-black undercoat tipped with white. These guinea pigs have dark eyes with a reddish cast.
- **Tortoiseshell**—Patches of red hair and patches of black hair make up an uneven checkerboard pattern over the bodies of tortoiseshell guinea pigs. They have dark eyes.
- **Tortoiseshell and white**—These guinea pigs have patches of red, black, and white hair that alternate from one side of the animal to the other. Their eyes are dark.
- **White**—This is a pure white with no brassy or yellow tinge. The eyes are either pink or a dark color.

This guinea pig is a silver agouti.

Popular Breeds

Thirteen breeds of domesticated guinea pigs are recognized by the American Rabbit Breeders Association, the official registry for guinea pigs in the United States. Each breed is a wonder in and of itself, unique in color, body type, and coat from all the others. Some have short, round bodies. Others have longer, more streamlined figures. Coat color, patterns, markings, and texture are different in each breed. Each of these breeds is available in the agouti, self, solid, and marked varieties.

Abyssinian The Abyssinian guinea pig is one of the oldest breeds. His coat is covered with rosettes, a pattern made up of radiated hair growing from a center point. The rosettes are placed one on each shoulder, four over the back, one on each hip, and two across the guinea pig's rear. The coat of the Abyssinian is coarse and dense and measures around one and a half inches long. The Abyssinian has a medium body length with rounded sides and plenty of depth to the shoulders and hindquarters.

Abyssinian

Abyssinian Satin The Abyssinian Satin has a shiny coat, as his name suggests. He is covered with rosettes exactly like those of the Abyssinian.

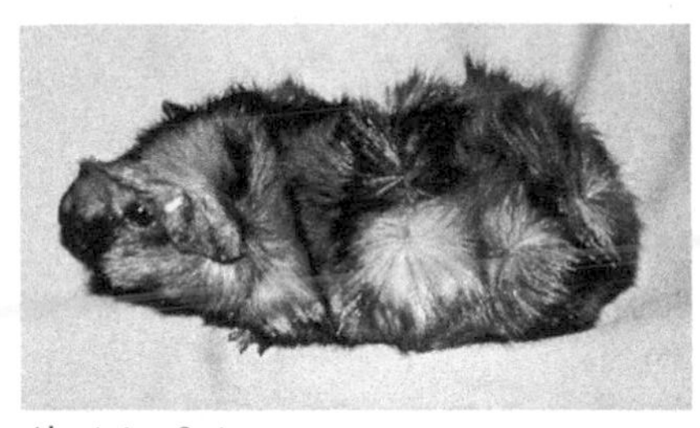
Abyssinian Satin

American The American is the most popular breed of guinea pig and has the appearance most people think of when they imagine a typical guinea pig. He has a Roman, or rounded, nose with ears that stick out from the sides of his head. His smooth coat lies close to his body.

American

American Satin The American Satin is the same as the American guinea pig, except that his coat is shiny and sleek.

American Satin

Coronet The Coronet has a long coat with a large rosette—or coronet—that runs from the tip of his nose to the center of his ears. The ears droop slightly.

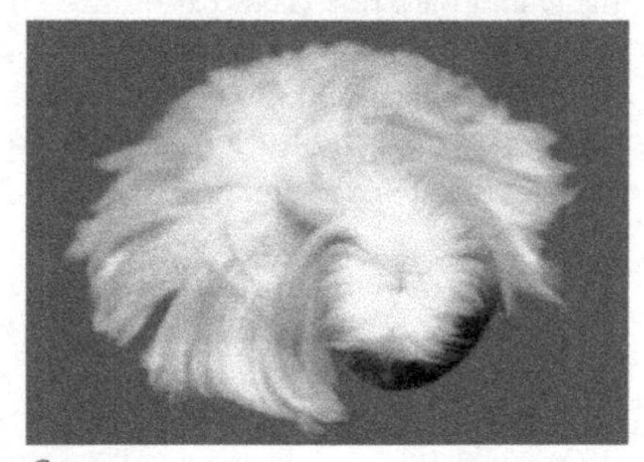
Coronet

Peruvian The Peruvian used to be known as the Angora. This breed has a long, sweeping coat that drags on the ground. The Peruvian's hair, which grows from a center part down the animal's back, is very dense and soft and requires a lot of grooming. Peruvian guinea pigs do best if their long hair is trimmed, for ease in grooming and so the animal can see where he is going.

Peruvian

Peruvian Satin The Peruvian Satin is very similar to the Peruvian, except that his coat is much silkier and more lustrous.

Peruvian Satin

Silkie The Silkie (known as the Sheltie in Britain) is so named because of the softness of his very long hair. The hair grows back from the guinea pig's nose and over his back in a teardrop pattern. Because of his luxurious coat, the Silkie requires a lot of grooming.

Silkie

Silkie Satin The only difference between the Silkie and the Silkie Satin is the coat. The Silkie Satin's hair is very long, dense, and lustrous like the Silkie's, but it has a distinctive sheen.

Silkie Satin

Teddy The Teddy was developed from a mutation. The breed has a dense, resilient, kinky coat that is about three-quarters of an inch long. Two different textures are seen in the Teddy's coat: plush, which is soft; and harsh, which is rough.

Teddy

Teddy Satin Like the Teddy, the Teddy Satin has a short, dense, kinky coat, although it will reveal a glowing sheen in the right lighting.

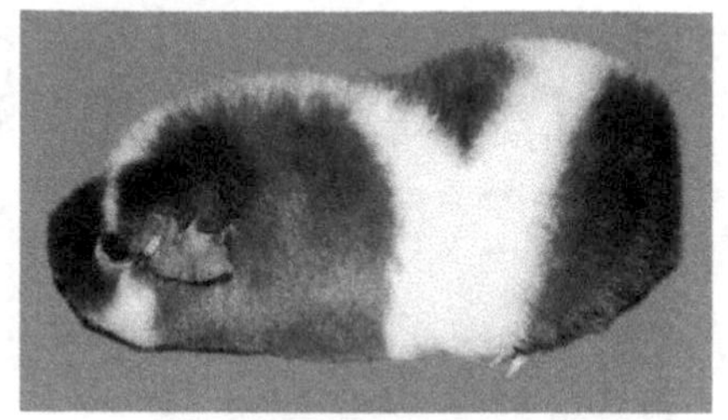

Teddy Satin

Texel The Texel is the newest breed recognized by the American Rabbit Breeders Association. The Texel's unique coat of ringlets or curls sets him apart from other cavy breeds.

Texel

White Crested The White Crested has a single white rosette atop his head. This marking is very difficult to breed for, and consequently, there are not many show-quality White Cresteds around today. A correct crest is centered on a line running from the tip of the guinea pig's nose to the center of his ears. In a show-quality White Crested, there are no other white hairs on the body.

White Crested

d Is Born

Breeders Association (ARBA) cur- breeds of cavies, this number is not ...ally admits new breeds that meet the orga- ...ent requirements for recognition.

...w type of guinea pig to be considered a recognized ...ed by ARBA, the proposed new breed must possess unique individual characteristics that are separate from those of other breeds. The cavies in question must also be able to pass these characteristics on to all of their offspring.

Once breeding consistency has been established, the person or persons who developed this new breed must follow a complicated procedure set forth by ARBA for breed recognition. First, the breeder must acquire a certificate of development from ARBA and provide proof of interest from five or more ARBA members, indicating that they are actively striving to produce guinea pigs that meet a proposed written standard.

Next, the breeder must present the breed to the ARBA standards committee for review at the next ARBA convention. The breed must be exhibited three times successfully at ARBA conventions before it can move on to the next stage of approval.

After the three presentations and approval from the ARBA standards committee, the breed standard is presented to the ARBA president, who presents the breed to the ARBA board of directors. If a majority of the board approves, the breed is added to the ARBA list of recognized cavy breeds.

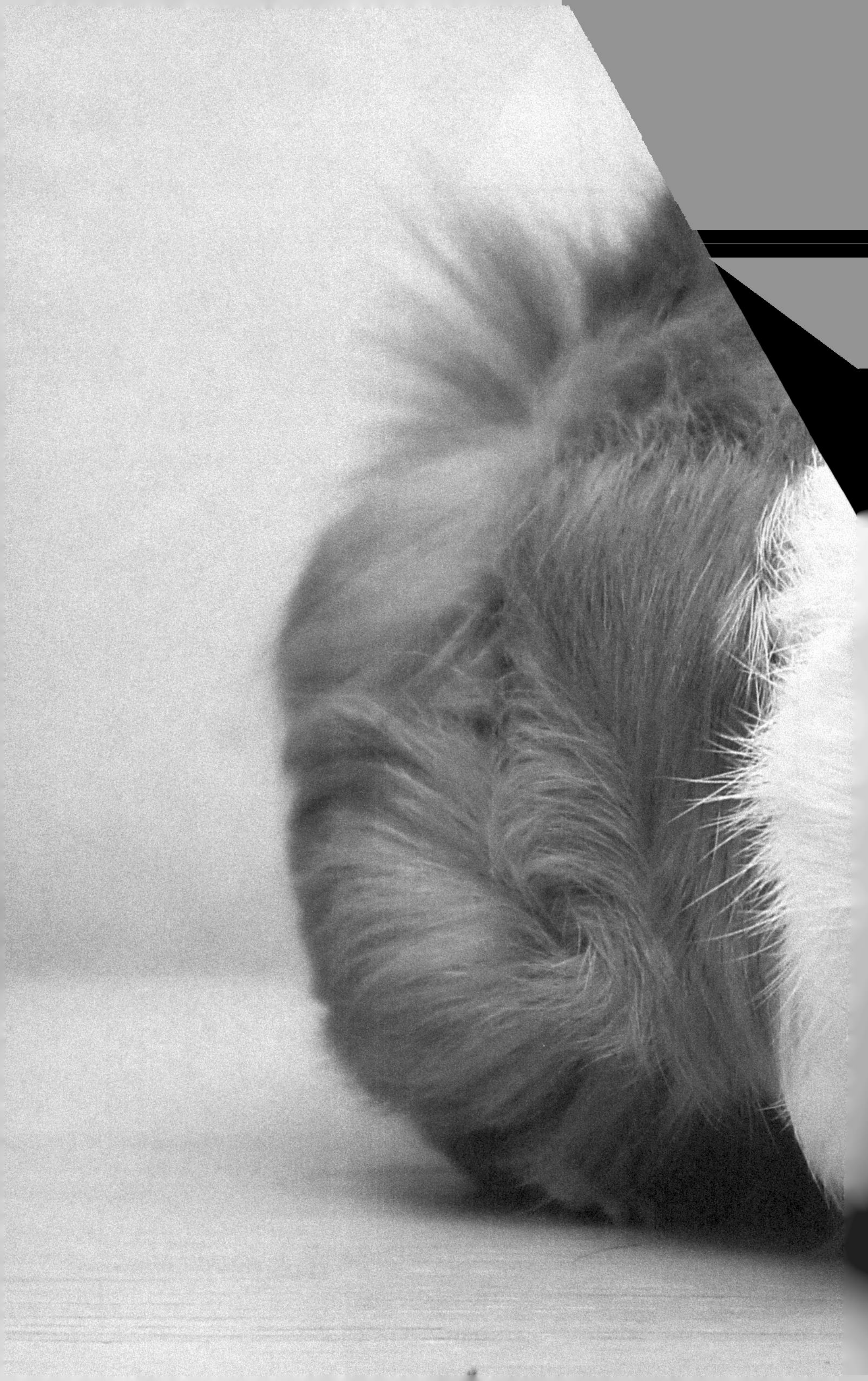

Part II

Caring for Your Guinea Pig

Chapter 4

Choosing Your Guinea Pig

When you're ready for your guinea pig, you'll want to start out on the right foot by looking for your new companion in the best way possible. You can buy a guinea pig from a pet store or a breeder, or you can adopt one. There are pros and cons to all these choices.

Adoption

If you are simply looking for a pet guinea pig, one to share your life and be a companion, consider adoption. Just as with dogs and cats, homeless guinea pigs are in desperate need of loving families. Every day, unwanted guinea pigs are being put to death at animal shelters all over the country simply because nobody wants them.

Guinea pigs in need of adoption are usually hapless creatures who once belonged to a family. They may have been purchased on an impulse or were the result of an unplanned litter. Through no fault of their own, they are later discarded. They deserve a second chance with a family who will love them and care for them throughout their lives.

If you would like to provide a home for a guinea pig who is desperately in need of one, there are several ways to go about it. First, call animal shelters in your area and ask if they have any guinea pigs available for adoption. If you stop by the shelter in person and do not see any guinea pigs, be sure to ask if any are available, since many shelters keep guinea pigs in a back room away from the dogs and cats. Adopting a guinea pig directly from a shelter means you will be saving a life.

Private shelters and rescue groups also seek homes for guinea pigs. The Internet can be a good source for rescue groups in your area. Most rabbit rescue groups also place guinea pigs, so search for rabbit rescue organizations in your area. (If you can't locate one of these groups through the Internet, call a local veterinarian who specializes in treating exotic animals. They may be able to refer you to a local group.)

If you choose to adopt from a rescue organization, be prepared to answer a lot of questions when you call. Rescue groups seeking to place a guinea pig in a new home have the responsibility to ask questions about the potential adoptive home to determine if the situation is right for both the guinea pig and the new owner.

When adopting through a shelter or rescue group, you may also be asked to pay a small adoption fee. This is usually done to weed out unscrupulous people who may only be looking for a free guinea pig to feed to a pet reptile or to use for some other unsavory purpose. Adoption fees also help guinea pig rescuers offset the costs of caring for homeless guinea pigs until new owners are found.

With so many homeless guinea pigs, adopting one will make you and your new pet feel great.

If you can't find a rescue group in your area and your shelter does not have any guinea pigs available, check the classified ads in your local newspaper, as well as bulletin boards in supermarkets, veterinarians' offices, and pet supply stores to find local people seeking homes for guinea pigs.

When conducting your adoption search, you will undoubtedly come across nonpurebred guinea pigs in need of homes. Consider bringing one of these guinea pigs into your life. Mixed breeds are often attractive guinea pigs and have an interesting quality that most purebreds don't: Each one is truly unique. If you have your heart set on a purebred guinea pig, look for a purebred in need of rescue. Many purebred guinea pigs also need good homes.

Buying a Guinea Pig

If you want to buy a guinea pig, it's important to not make the decision impulsively. All pets need and deserve a commitment from their owners. Guinea pigs can live as long as seven years. The adorable baby guinea pig in the window may be tiny and cute now, but in a few months she will be a large adult who will need years of consistent, thoughtful care. Buying a pet on an impulse often results in unhappiness for the owner and a sorry fate for the animal.

Breeders

If you are absolutely sure you want to own a guinea pig, the best place to buy one is from a responsible breeder. Responsible breeders are guinea pig fanciers who research bloodlines before breeding their guinea pigs and who keep their animals in clean and healthy environments. They are experts on their breed of choice and frequently show their animals. And if you think you might like to show your pet, you must have an animal with the pedigree that only a breeder can provide.

Purebred Pedigree

If you are buying a purebred guinea pig from a breeder, ask them for a signed pedigree. This document will state your guinea pig's sex, color, and parentage. You may later choose to register your guinea pig with the American Rabbit Breeders Association if you want to show the animal at local guinea pig shows.

Responsible breeders are experts on their breed of choice.

Buying your pet from a responsible breeder will help ensure that you are obtaining the breed of guinea pig that is best for you because each breed has its own special qualities. If you buy a young, purebred guinea pig from a breeder, you will know exactly what she will look like when she matures. You can also see one or both of your pet's parents, giving you the opportunity to see what their personalities are like since their offspring are likely to have similar temperaments.

A responsible breeder will welcome you, as a prospective buyer, into their breeding operation, allowing you to see firsthand the environment the guinea pig has been living in. This way, you will be able to gauge whether your prospective pet has been well cared for and is living in clean and healthy conditions.

Buying from a breeder also offers an added bonus: You go home with the name and phone number of an experienced person who can answer your questions and provide you with help in raising your guinea pig. If you are interested in showing your guinea pig, the breeder can help you get started in that area, too.

Once you have determined the breed you want, you can obtain the name and phone number of a breeder in your area by contacting one of the regional clubs in your area or by getting in touch with the American Cavy Breeders Association (see the appendix). Another way to find a guinea pig breeder is to attend a local rabbit and cavy show. Walk around, look at the different guinea pig breeds, and speak to some of the exhibitors. Let people know you are looking to buy a guinea pig from a breeder, and they will direct you to the appropriate individuals.

Breeders may have several animals you can choose from.

Your local 4-H group is another possible source for breeders. Call the local county extension office (listed in your telephone book), and ask for the name and number of a 4-H guinea pig leader in your area. This person should be able to put you in touch with a breeder nearby.

Pet Stores

Many people buy guinea pigs from pet stores. If you choose to purchase your pet from a retailer, make sure the store environment is clean and that the guinea pigs and other small animals are healthy and well-kept. Be sure to get a health guarantee on any animal you purchase.

Things to Consider When Choosing Your Guinea Pig

Age

Age is not a very important factor when buying a guinea pig, as long as the animal has been handled from a young age. Adult guinea pigs can make wonderful pets. Since guinea pigs usually live anywhere from five to seven years, you can adopt or purchase a guinea pig who is several years old and still have a lot of time left to spend with her.

If your heart is set on getting a baby guinea pig, make sure the one you buy is at least 4 weeks old. Young guinea pigs should stay with their mothers until they are a month old. Taking them away too soon can be damaging both emotionally and physically, and guinea pigs removed from their mothers' care too early rarely survive for long once they arrive in their new homes.

Health

It's important to start out on the right foot by selecting a guinea pig who is in good health. A guinea pig's general health can be determined in a number of ways. Check to see if her ears and nose are clean and free of discharge and debris. Then take a close look at her fur. The fur of a healthy guinea pig will be soft, shiny, and even. Keep an eye out for lice in the ears and fur, bald spots, and signs of diarrhea. Check around the cage to make sure that the guinea pig's fecal pellets are round and hard; diarrhea is a sign of illness.

Feel the guinea pig's body. It should be round, tight, and smooth. If the abdomen is hard and round, the guinea pig may be suffering from a worm infestation.

If you have your heart set on a baby, make sure she is at least 4 weeks old.

The health of your guinea pig is a top concern. She should look clean and alert and feel solid.

Attitude is also important when determining a guinea pig's health. Look for an animal who is bright eyed, alert, and active. A guinea pig who appears dull and listless is probably sick.

Be sure to take notice of the guinea pig's surroundings. Are they clean and relatively odor free? Are the animals kept in spacious, airy cages? Do the other guinea pigs appear healthy? Many guinea pig diseases are contagious. If the guinea pig you are considering for purchase is housed near a sick guinea pig, chances are your pet will come down with the same illness.

Check the guinea pig's teeth to see if the two top teeth overlap the two lower teeth. Do not buy a guinea pig whose upper incisors do not overlap the lower incisors. This condition is called malocclusion and is a serious problem in guinea pigs that can result in much grief to both guinea pig and owner. Misaligned teeth do not wear down properly and can grow out of control. Unless they are regularly trimmed by a veterinarian, they will cause mouth infections and jaw problems, and can even grow so long that they will curve back into the guinea pig's skull and kill the animal.

If you are buying your pet from a breeder, talk to them about the guinea pig you are considering. Ask questions about the animal's ancestors. What were their personalities like? Did they have any health problems that could be genetic? If you plan to show your guinea pig, ask about the show careers of the guinea pig's parents and grandparents. Ask to see the guinea pig's sire (father) and dam (mother). Study the standard (a description of the ideal guinea pig) for the breed you are considering and try to apply it to the guinea pig's parents. If they are good specimens of the breed, chances are their offspring will be, too.

While you are discussing the guinea pig with the breeder or retailer, ask them if they have a return policy if the guinea pig becomes ill. If you have other pets, particularly a dog, also find out if the seller will take the guinea pig back if your other pets will not accept her into the household.

Personality

If you give your guinea pig love and attention, chances are she will become a wonderful pet. However, when you are selecting your guinea pig, you may want to observe the personality of the animals you are considering to see which one strikes your fancy. Guinea pigs who appear nervous and afraid may be high-strung or just unused to being handled. If the animal is young, she is still very impressionable and will learn to be held and stroked if you show her love and consideration. Older guinea pigs who have not been handled much will need more work to make them comfortable with people. Eventually, though, they should learn to respond to care and affection.

Gender

Debate goes on in guinea pig circles over which make better pets: males (boars) or females (sows). The answer really depends on what you plan to do with your cavy.

Females are said to be mainly concerned with reproducing. They emit an odor and are very interested in breeding with males that they meet. Males, on

Naming Your Guinea Pig

Once you choose your guinea pig, you will need to name her. If you have children, let them participate in choosing the name. You can get inspiration from the guinea pig's color (Blackie), or shape (Peanut), or personality (Snuggles). Whatever you do, don't choose something that's ugly or unkind. You will be using your guinea pig's name for years to come, so make sure it's an attractive name that bears repeating.

Spaying and Neutering

Worries about gender and reproduction can be solved very simply by spaying and neutering. Pet guinea pigs who will not be shown or bred should be spayed or neutered. Once this is done, their troublesome hormones will disappear, they will be healthier, and you will have a gentler, loving pet. Preventing your pet from having a litter will also help curb the guinea pig overpopulation problem, meaning fewer guinea pigs in animal shelters will lose their lives.

the other hand, are thought to be somewhat aggressive and unsettled. They also have a strong odor and will be territorial with other males.

If you decide to spay or neuter your guinea pig, however, gender should not be a factor in your purchasing decision, since spayed sows and neutered boars make equally good pets.

If you plan to get two guinea pigs who will live together in the same cage, make sure you have accurate information about the animals' gender. If you have more than one guinea pig and you do not want to spay or neuter them, you will need to get two females. There is no way to stop a male and a female from breeding, and two unneutered males will fight with each other. The problem is that male and female guinea pigs can be hard to tell apart, especially when they are young. Get expert advice from a breeder or veterinarian about the gender of your pets before you place them together.

Chapter 5

Bringing Your Guinea Pig Home

You've chosen the guinea pig you are going to adopt or buy. Before you bring him home, though, you need to prepare his environment. Shopping for and setting up all the equipment and supplies you'll need for your guinea pig *before* his arrival will make his introduction to your home less stressful for both of you.

Indoors or Outdoors?

Before you get a guinea pig, you should decide whether your pet will live inside your home with you or outdoors in the yard. Indoors is best, for all the reasons I will explain. However, guinea pigs can live either indoors or outside, and the items you'll need to have on hand before your pet's arrival will vary somewhat depending on where your guinea pig will live.

It's impossible to truly appreciate life with a guinea pig unless you keep him inside your home. Just like dogs and cats, guinea pigs are companion animals with unique and interesting personalities. If you don't actually live with a guinea pig, day in and day out, you'll never really get to know him. The guinea pig won't get to know you that well, either.

If your guinea pig is outside most of the time, the two of you will lead separate lives. You'll miss out on the chance to have him sleep on your lap while you watch television and gaze up at you from the floor while you eat your dinner. People who live with indoor guinea pigs enjoy these antics and more from their pets.

It's impossible to truly appreciate life with a guinea pig unless you keep him inside with you.

There are many other practical reasons for keeping a guinea pig indoors. Guinea pigs who stay inside tend to live longer than outdoor guinea pigs. Bad weather and predators are responsible for the demise of many outdoor guinea pigs. These are consequences of outdoor living that even conscientious owners can't always control.

Illness is a major cause of death among outdoor guinea pigs, mostly because outdoor pets are more difficult to monitor. Signs of sickness can be subtle at first, and since outdoor guinea pigs spend less time with their owners, it can be a day or so before the owner recognizes the illness. In the case of rapidly progressing illnesses, a delay of even one day can cost a guinea pig his life.

The decision to keep your guinea pig indoors is a wise one. Even guinea pigs who have been living outside for years can acclimate to a life indoors.

Indoor Housing

Even though your indoor guinea pig will have the same roof over his head that you do, he'll still need his own private retreat. A cage will offer security for your guinea pig (and your home!) and can also give him privacy and a safe haven.

Indoor guinea pig cages are available in pet supply stores and through catalogs, and there are a wide variety of styles. Look for one made from sturdy wire, with a removable bottom tray. Your guinea pig will not be able to gnaw on the wire, and the removable tray will make cleaning easier. Wire will also give your pet the ventilation and light he needs.

A solid, rustproof metal or hard plastic floor is suitable for a guinea pig. While a wire mesh bottom can make cage cleaning easier, it is not very safe for your guinea pig because his legs can easily get caught in it. Also, wire floors can result in sore feet and hocks. If you insist on a cage with a wire floor, a solid area made of wood (any type except redwood, which is toxic) must be provided somewhere in the cage so the guinea pig can find relief from the wire bottom.

The indoor cage should be big enough for the guinea pig to stretch out and move around in while also accommodating a nest box, food and water accessories, and a toy or two. The height of the cage should allow the guinea pig to stand up on his hind legs without his head touching the top.

Look for a cage that is sturdily constructed and easy to disassemble for cleaning. It should also have a door on top so you can reach inside and a door on the side so the guinea pig can go in and out of the cage when he wishes.

Nest Box

Guinea pigs are burrowing animals by nature. In the wild, they live under the ground in dens they dig themselves. These burrows provide them with a sense of security. For this reason, guinea pigs who live above ground as pets enjoy having nest boxes, a substitute for burrows, inside their cage.

A nest box is a small enclosure that contains the animal's bedding and has an entry hole cut into it. It provides a safe place to sleep and hide. A cardboard box would work well as a nest box, but most guinea pigs will quickly chew it to pieces, so wood is preferred. (They'll chew that, too, but not as fast.)

Commercially made nest boxes are available through pet supply outlets and mail-order catalogs that specialize in small animal supplies. Or you can build your own. Just make sure the wood has never been treated with anything toxic.

Guinea pigs get a sense of security when they have small places they can retreat into.

Your guinea pig's nest box should be big enough for the animal to turn around in while several inches of bedding are in place. Make sure the entrance to the nest box is big enough for your guinea pig to go in easily and that one side of the box is removable so you can clean it. There should be no sharp edges anywhere in the box.

Location

When you are deciding where in the house to put your guinea pig's cage, remember that extreme temperatures are dangerous for these animals. Do not put your guinea pig's cage in a spot where the sun will shine directly on it. Avoid keeping it near a radiator, stove, fireplace, or other heating element.

Cold drafts can also be deadly. Keep your guinea pig's cage away from doors and windows, where winter drafts can leak in. Try to keep your guinea pig's cage off the floor during cold weather, too, since cold air tends to lie near the ground, creating drafts.

Avoid placing your guinea pig's cage in dark or damp areas. Basements and garages are not suitable areas for guinea pigs since they typically have mini-

When your guinea pig is out of his cage, you'll have to make sure the room he's in is safe.

mal light, poor ventilation, and excessive moisture. Garages are also dangerous because guinea pigs are sensitive to car-exhaust fumes.

Try to find a place in your home where your guinea pig will be able to watch the household activity without being unduly disturbed. You want your guinea pig to feel like part of the family, so his cage needs to be in a room where people come and go. However, don't put him in such a busy spot that he will never be able to rest or relax. Be especially careful not to place the cage near a television set, stereo, or radio. A guinea pig's hearing is very sensitive, and a lot of noise can be very disturbing.

Guinea Pig Proofing

Because guinea pigs are gnawing animals and have an innate need to chew, it is vitally important that you guinea pig proof your home before you let your pet run loose. Along with providing your guinea pig with toys he can chew on, you'll also need to devise ways to keep him from gnawing on household items, for the sake of your home and the animal's health.

Electrical cords pose the greatest threat to your guinea pig's safety and should be a primary concern. Guinea pigs will chew through cords, electrocuting themselves and creating a fire hazard in your home. You can protect your home and your guinea pig by moving dangling cords out of reach. Cords that cannot be moved should be covered with plastic aquarium-type tubing. To do this, slit the tubing lengthwise and lay the cord inside. Or try wrapping the cord with spiral cable wrap, available in electronics stores.

Guinea pigs will chew on anything made of wood, so wooden moldings, furniture legs, and other chewables that will be attractive to your guinea pig can be covered with thick plastic or treated with a scent deterrent. Perfume and cologne are repugnant to guinea pigs, who have a sharp sense of smell. You can also use store-bought repellents made to keep away other pets. Not all guinea pigs will be rebuffed by this, however, and you may have to resort to covering areas with unchewable surfaces.

Another important aspect to guinea pig proofing your home is to take a survey of all the places where your guinea pig could get caught or hide. Since guinea pigs are inquisitive animals, your pet will want to explore every nook and cranny of your house. Look around for guinea pig–size spaces that your pet can escape through or get trapped in. Block off these areas securely. And while you are surveying the house, make sure that toxic household chemicals and trash bags are well hidden from your pet.

Guinea Pig Proofing Your Home

You can prevent much of the destruction guinea pigs can cause and keep your new pet safe by looking at your home from a guinea pig's point of view. Get down on all fours and look around. Do you see loose electrical wires, cords dangling from the blinds, chewy shoes on the floor? Your guinea pig will see them, too!

In all the rooms your guinea pig will be allowed in:

- Get plastic trashcans with tight-fitting lids.
- Spray wooden moldings and furniture legs with a scent deterrent, or cover them with a nonchewable surface.
- Keep all household cleaners, medicines, vitamins, shampoos, bath products, perfumes, makeup, nail polish remover, and other personal products in cupboards that close securely.
- Cover or tack up electrical cords; consider childproof covers for unused outlets.
- Knot or tie up any dangling cords from curtains, blinds, and the telephone.
- Put all houseplants out of reach.
- Pick up all chewable items, including television and electronics remote controls, cellphones, shoes, socks, slippers and sandals, food, dishes, cups and utensils, toys, books and magazines, and anything else that can be chewed on.
- Block off all nooks, cracks, and crevices where a guinea pig could hide.

Outdoor Housing

If keeping your guinea pig indoors is out of the question, it is possible to successfully house him outside if you take strict precautions. Before you prepare to bring your outdoor guinea pig home with you, be sure to check your local zoning ordinances to make certain it is legal to keep a guinea pig outdoors in your area.

When determining what kind of housing you will provide for your guinea pig and where it will be located, there are many details you must keep in mind so your guinea pig will be healthy and safe. You will need to protect your guinea pig from the elements, as well as from extreme changes in temperature. You will also need to guard against predators and give your guinea pig enough room to move around comfortably.

Hutch Size

There are a number of commercially made hutches that are suitable for guinea pigs. It's important to choose a hutch that will meet your guinea pig's needs for shelter, comfort, and safety.

First, consider size. The more room you can provide for your guinea pig, the better. Buy your guinea pig the largest hutch your space will accommodate. Giving your guinea pig plenty of room to move around will help him stay happy and healthy.

When you're thinking about the hutch, keep your pet's size in mind. In general, each adult guinea pig will need a minimum of a hundred square inches of floor space, and more is better. A guinea pig who does not have enough room in his hutch may become depressed. A space that's too small will be fouled more quickly with feces and urine, leaving the guinea pig to spend more time than he should in unsanitary conditions and making cleanup a bigger hassle for you. (But don't get a single-door hutch that is so deep you can't reach into it to clean it. Large hutches should have more than one door.)

You'll also want to make sure that the hutch is big enough to accommodate a separate sleeping space, either a nest box or a built-in compartment. Providing your guinea pig with a secluded and separate place to sleep will help him feel

The hutch should be made of sturdy wood and have plenty of space. Guinea pigs need more room than you might think.

safer and happier in the hutch. A built-in sleeping compartment should be about eighteen inches long and six inches high and wide.

Larger hutches can also accommodate litter boxes. If you'd like your guinea pig to spend time free roaming with you inside your home, you may want to try to litter box train him and then have him use a litter box even in his hutch. This way, he will be used to using the box and will be less likely to have an accident when he is in the house.

Hutch Materials

Most hutches are made from either wood and wire or metal. Each has its advantages and disadvantages. Wooden hutches usually consist of a wooden roof and wood-panel sides, with wire mesh on the door, front, and/or some sides of the cage. Wooden hutches stay cooler in the summer and warmer in the winter, as long as they are made with a good quality wood and not pressboard. They can also be very attractive.

One problem with wooden hutches is that the wood can eventually rot, causing the hutch to slowly fall apart. Another disadvantage is that guinea pigs love to chew on wood and can gnaw sections of a wooden hutch to pieces if the wood is not protected by wire mesh.

Metal hutches retain heat in the summer and cold in the winter, which can be harmful to the guinea pig inside. They are very durable, however, and can last a very long time if they are well made. They are also easier to clean than wood hutches and often are less expensive.

Whether you choose a wooden hutch or a metal hutch, it's important to select a home for your guinea pig that uses the proper type of wire. Chicken wire is not acceptable, since it is flimsy and is easily removed by both predators and the guinea pigs themselves. Side panels and doors on both wooden and metal hutches should be made from sturdy, galvanized wire, around 14-gauge in weight. The size of the holes in the wire mesh should be no larger than one inch by two inches.

Improper flooring can really hurt your guinea pig. Wire mesh is easy to clean, but it can be dangerous.

The roof of an outdoor hutch should be covered with a waterproof substance, such as heavy-duty plastic or roofing material. This is vital if the hutch and its occupant are to stay warm and dry.

The floor is very important because improper flooring can cause a number of health problems in your guinea pig. Most hutches have some wire flooring, designed to allow feces and urine to drop away from the animal. However, wire mesh that is too large can be dangerous because a guinea pig's leg can fall through. The wire mesh should also be smooth because rough edges can result in sore hocks.

Make sure at least one-third of the floor space contains a flat, porous surface (preferably wood) where your guinea pig can sit to get off the wire. This is important because constant walking on wire can cause sore hocks.

Hutch Design

When considering which hutch to get for an outdoor guinea pig, the most important factors are your guinea pig's health, safety, and comfort. Beyond this, there are some decisions to make about convenience, quality, and aesthetic appeal.

The first feature to look at in hutch design is quality. Does the hutch appear to be well built? Is it made from quality materials? Look to see that the welding was done before the metal was galvanized. (Welds should be under the rustproof coating, not over it.) Check the hinges and various connections throughout the hutch to see if they are well put together. Examine the construction carefully to make sure the hutch is secure and escape proof. Feel around for sharp points. Unfinished edges indicate sloppy craftsmanship and a danger to your guinea pig.

Another element to consider is height. Some hutches are low to the ground, while others have legs that put them anywhere from several inches to several feet up. Cages should not rest directly on the ground. For better ventilation and sanitation, hutches should be at least six inches off the ground. Hutches that rest directly on soil may end up being homes for mice and rats, who will create nests underneath the floor. If you buy a hutch with no legs, you'll have to raise it up off the ground some other way. It's best if the bottom of the cage is waist high. This makes the hutch easier to clean and makes access to the guinea pig less difficult for you.

When it comes to convenience, the location and style of doors are also important factors in hutch design. Outdoor hutches usually have doors on the front of the cage, although some will have top-opening entries. Unless your hutch is very low to the ground, you will want to buy a design that has a door in the front. This will make it easier to reach in for cleaning.

TIP

Keeping Cool

To protect your guinea pig from overheating in the summertime, put plastic jugs of frozen water in the hutch that your guinea pig can lie against to keep cool. Keep a few of these jugs in your freezer so you can rotate them.

To ensure that the hutch fits the needs of their pets, many guinea pig owners will design and build their own outdoor hutches. If you choose to do this, you may want to contact your local county extension office or the American Rabbit Breeders Association for plans and further information on how to construct a safe and sturdy hutch.

Location

Heat is more dangerous to guinea pigs than cold, so when choosing a location for the hutch, make sure it is in a shady spot. This is particularly important if you live in a warm climate. Wild guinea pigs live underground in burrows. Exposing them to direct sun or extreme heat can easily kill them. Temperatures above 85 degrees are considered dangerous for guinea pigs, especially if the humidity is also high.

On the other hand, you don't want to keep your guinea pig in cold and darkness. In fact, guinea pigs need long periods of light in order to sleep since they are nocturnal. The location you pick must get indirect sunlight that does not shine directly on the hutch.

Guinea pigs need to be protected from damp and drafts.

Indoors or out, you need to place your guinea pig's home in a spot where the temperature will not fluctuate rapidly.

While guinea pigs are more able to tolerate the cold, they should be protected from drafts. Guinea pigs who are subjected to constant wind or drafts will eventually become sick, because their immune systems will be compromised by the stress on their bodies. Choose a protected location for your guinea pig hutch, out of drafts and wind. Placing a hutch alongside a building can often provide defense from the wind.

Dampness is a killer of guinea pigs, and you must make sure your pet stays dry. Hot, humid weather can cause moldy, unsanitary conditions in the nesting box, and rain or snow can drench a guinea pig and his entire bed. Even though your hutch will have a waterproof roof, you must place it in a location where it will be sheltered from wind-driven rain and snow and excessive dampness.

Temperatures that rise and fall rapidly in short periods of time are not good for guinea pigs, either. If you live in a climate where the days are hot and the nights are cold, your outdoor guinea pig will suffer. Since there is little you can do to protect an outdoor guinea pig from these kinds of temperature extremes, it is best to keep your pet's cage indoors during the harshest times of the year.

Ventilation is also an important factor in hutch placement. Caged guinea pigs need plenty of fresh air, because a stuffy environment can wreak havoc on a guinea pig's respiratory system. The ammonia from the guinea pig's urine and the dust from his bedding can cause respiratory distress and infection, causing the animal to become sick and even die. Make sure you select a spot that is well ventilated while still protected from the elements.

Don't place the hutch in a spot where there is excessive noise. Guinea pigs need to sleep during the day and will become nervous and stressed if there are frequent loud noises or disturbances.

When choosing a spot for your guinea pig's home, keep in mind that you will need to have convenient access to it so you can clean it regularly, give food to your guinea pig, and take your guinea pig out daily for exercise and companionship.

It is vital to always remember that guinea pigs are prey animals and will attract any number of predators. Dogs and cats are only two of the creatures that will be drawn to your yard once a guinea pig is in place. Depending on where you live, raccoons, coyotes, hawks, foxes, owls, and even weasels may try to get to your guinea pig. Providing a secure hutch does not necessarily mean that your guinea pig will be safe. Raccoons are known to prey on small mammals and can reach through the wire of a hutch and kill a guinea pig. Other animals can kill your guinea pig by frightening him to death even though they can't actually get at him. Guinea pigs can go into fatal shock from fear alone.

It's difficult to provide an outdoor guinea pig with both physical and psychological protection from predators without actually building an enclosed fence around his hutch. However, if you want to ensure that your guinea pig is safe from other animals, you will need to do this. The idea behind the enclosure is not only to keep predators from gaining access to your guinea pig's hutch, but also to keep them far enough away so that they don't frighten your guinea pig.

A guinea pig hutch can be kept on an apartment terrace, as long as the space is protected in the same ways as a backyard. Provide shade for the hutch and safeguards from climbing predators, as well as protection from drafts and temperature extremes.

Outdoor Guinea Pig Care

Guinea pigs who are housed outdoors need special attention. Because your guinea pig is not living inside with you, you will need to make an extra effort to observe him and spend time with him. You will also have to make sure his outdoor environment is well tended.

Good and Bad Plants

The following are some plants that you must take care not to let your guinea pig have access to:

- Daffodil
- Tulip
- Lily of the valley

On the other hand, some plants are downright tasty and nutritious for your guinea pig. Consider allowing him small portions of these as a treat:

- Clover
- Dandelions
- Mallow
- Shepherd's purse
- Yarrow

Observation

One of the most important aspects of outdoor guinea pig care is observation. Because signs of illness can often be subtle at the onset of a disease, it is vital that you keep a close watch on your guinea pig. Early treatment of an illness can often mean the difference between life and death. Learn to know how your pet behaves when he is feeling good so you can immediately recognize when there is a problem. Check on him frequently throughout the day to see how he is doing.

Exercise

It's important that your guinea pig get daily exercise. If you cannot bring him inside the house to play, you'll have to provide him with a completely enclosed run in the backyard to stretch his legs (the bigger the better, with four feet being the minimum length). Or use an empty plastic wading pool and let your pet run around in it and play with his toys.

An outdoor guinea pig will still need a lot of play time with you.

If your yard is enclosed by walls or a sturdy fence with no holes that a guinea pig can slip through, you may give your pet the run of the yard. However, a guinea pig should never run loose without supervision, since he may fall victim to a predator (including birds such as owls or hawks who can swoop down from the sky) or poisonous plants in your yard.

Social Interaction

Since guinea pigs are highly social creatures, an outdoor guinea pig living alone in a hutch can suffer terribly from loneliness. For this reason, you will need to make a concerted effort to provide him with social interaction. Bring him in the house as often as you can so he can spend time with you. Sit in the backyard with him as he plays in his run or in the yard. And get another guinea pig to keep him company in his hutch.

Regular Cleaning

Outdoor hutches get dirty quickly, and for your guinea pig's health and well-being you'll need to clean the hutch frequently. While you can get away with not cleaning it every day, it wouldn't hurt to do so.

Before you clean the hutch, remove your guinea pig and put him in a safe place. (A travel carrier is useful for this purpose.) Don't let him roam about unsupervised; he may get into trouble while you are working.

Because guinea pigs normally live in dens, they tend to use the same area of their hutch all the time as a toilet. Using a spatula and hand shovel, scrape away the feces and urine that build up in that area. Once a week, scrub the area until it is clean using a hard-bristle brush and water containing a splash of bleach. Wait until the inside of the hutch is completely dry before placing the guinea pig back in.

While you are cleaning the hutch, use the opportunity to inspect the inside for damage or anything that needs repair.

Cage Amenities

Whether your guinea pig lives indoors or out, he will need more than just a cage to live a comfortable and healthy life. There are a number of cage accessories you should buy before his arrival.

Your guinea pig's food bowl is very important and should be chosen wisely. Don't use any old dish you have in the cupboard, as guinea pigs will chew up or knock over the wrong kind of food container. Instead, take a trip to your local pet supply store and buy a ceramic crock made specifically for pets. Ceramic crocks are chew resistant and difficult to knock over.

A crockery food dish is easy to clean. And don't forget the hay rack.

When you buy a food crock, keep your guinea pig's size in mind. Don't buy a dish that's too small for the guinea pig to put his head into or too big for him to reach into comfortably.

Another option is a metal bowl that attaches to the side of the cage. When selecting a metal bowl, be sure it's not so deep that the guinea pig can't reach all the way into it. Make sure the bowl is attached to the side of the cage at a low enough level to allow easy access.

Another necessity for your guinea pig's cage is a water bottle. Gravity water bottles are easy to find in pet supply stores. These are the best type of water containers for guinea pigs since they are impossible to knock over and the water stays clean in the bottle. Make sure the water bottle you buy is not too small (it should be larger than eight ounces). You want your guinea pig to drink as much water as possible to maintain his health, and a small bottle will need filling more than once a day. Also, make sure the water bottle has a metal ball in the tip. This will keep it from leaking into your guinea pig's cage.

A hay rack is another important item for the cage. Hay is a vital element in your guinea pig's daily diet. A hay rack will hold the hay in place so it doesn't get scattered throughout the cage. Hay racks are usually made of metal and will attach to the upper side of the cage. The guinea pig can pull strands of hay from the rack whenever he gets the urge to munch.

Newspaper and commercial bedding pellets make a good substrate for the cage. Wood shavings are also fine, but avoid cedar.

Your guinea pig will need lots of toys.

A supply of food should be on hand. Find out what your guinea pig has been eating in his previous home and begin by offering him these same items. If you need to change his diet, you'll have to do so over a period of a few weeks so as not to upset his digestion. (See chapter 6 for information on what to feed your guinea pig.)

You'll need a litter box and litter if you are planning to try to litter box train your guinea pig. A small litter box made for a cat can be good for a guinea pig, provided the box is not too large.

You'll want to have bedding available for your guinea pig as well. Guinea pigs enjoy sleeping on wood shavings, shredded paper, processed ground corn cob, and commercial bedding pellets. Wood shavings, shredded paper, corn cob, and bedding pellets made especially for small animals can be purchased in any pet supply shop. (Some experts believe cedar shavings can be detrimental to a guinea pig's respiratory system. Many guinea pig owners prefer to use other, less aromatic, bedding for their pets.)

Since guinea pigs are gnawing mammals, you'll need to have safe chewing blocks in your guinea pig's cage. Untreated wood can be used, but the safest items to give your guinea pig to gnaw on are commercially prepared wood blocks or chews, available at pet supply stores. These gnawing toys are available in a variety of colors and shapes, are made especially for animals who chew, and are safe and inexpensive.

Many people are surprised to learn that guinea pigs love to play with toys. A toy for a guinea pig can be anything from an empty toilet paper roll to a small cardboard box. Having a few items on hand when your guinea pig arrives will help him feel at home in his new environment. While he might not play with these items right away, he will appreciate their presence once he becomes acclimated to his new environment.

And More to Buy

A few other items should also be on hand before you bring your guinea pig home. First and foremost is a travel carrier. You'll need to get it before your guinea pig makes the trip home with you, since you may need it for the journey. A small, plastic, airline-approved cat carrier works best for guinea pigs. Make sure you line the carrier bottom with newspaper so the guinea pig won't slide around during the ride home.

Your carrier will come in handy for trips to the vet and for confining your guinea pig whenever you clean his cage or need to keep him temporarily in a small space. A good carrier is a wise investment.

Since guinea pigs need regular grooming, you'll also need a brush, a comb, and a nail trimmer. For more on these items, see chapter 7.

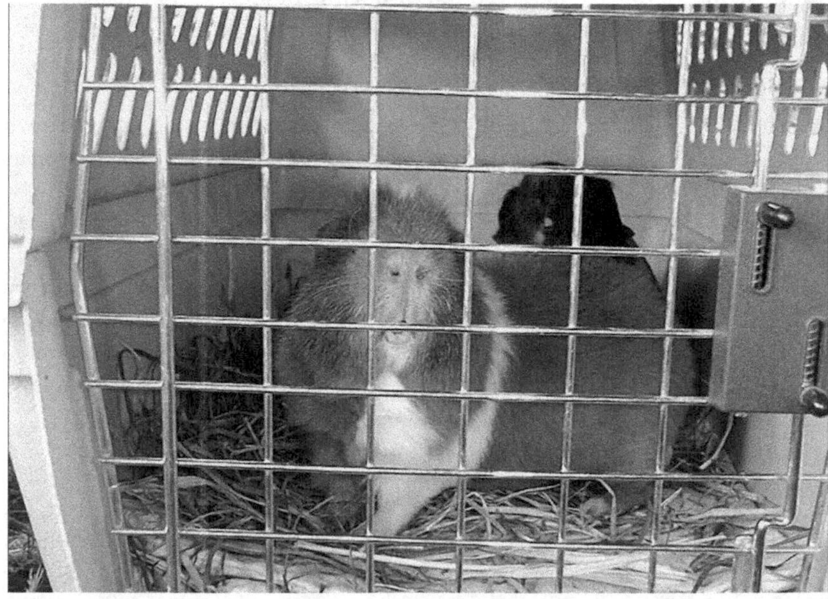

A carrier will be useful for trips and also as a safe place to stash your pet while you clean his cage.

Acclimating the Newcomer

When your new guinea pig comes home for the first time, it will be an exciting moment. Everyone in the family will be anxious to feel his soft fur and watch him investigate his new environment. As exhilarating as this moment will be, it is important to realize that your guinea pig will have a different perspective on the situation. Put yourself in his place for a moment: He's just been taken from his familiar surroundings, stuck in a box, and whisked away to a place he's never seen. Everything is new to him—and giant size! There's little doubt he will be overwhelmed.

Because of the guinea pig's instinct to always be alert for predators, you may notice that your new pet seems skittish and fearful. Remember that this is normal guinea pig behavior. Your pet will need a lot of love, patience, and understanding to learn to relax. Be sure to give him a place to hide when he is being introduced to his new situation. This will provide him with much-needed security.

The kindest way to let your guinea pig get used to his new home is to leave him alone for a while. Place him in his cage—which you equipped with food, water, and everything he'll need to survive—and then let him check things out in privacy for a couple of hours.

After your guinea pig has had a chance to get used to his new cage, you can begin to quietly observe him. Speak to him softly every so often to reassure him that everything is okay and to let him get used to your voice.

If you have children, this is a good time to start teaching them how to treat their new guinea pig. Explain to them that their new pet needs peace and quiet so he can learn to feel comfortable in his new home. If your children are anxious to show their new guinea pig to their friends, ask their friends to come in to visit one or two at a time so they don't scare the animal. They should be as quiet as possible when they are near the new pet. Guinea pigs' ears are very sensitive, and loud noises can be frightening.

Be sure your children understand that they should not handle the guinea pig right away. Because the new guinea pig will be fearful and skittish, any attempts to hold him may result in injury to the guinea pig. It's vital that you first learn the proper way to handle a guinea pig and then teach your child to do so. Once your child has learned handling techniques, always supervise to make sure it is being done correctly. A guinea pig's skeleton is fragile, and dropping a squirming guinea pig to the ground could result in fatal injury.

It's also important to keep other pets away from the new guinea pig while he is getting used to his surroundings. Your guinea pig needs time to adjust to his new life, and it is best to introduce him to each element one step at a time.

Your guinea pig may feel shy at first. Be patient and speak to him softly.

At first, keep his cage in an area that is somewhat secluded, where cats and dogs can't bother him. Later, when he is feeling more comfortable, you can have him meet your other pets.

Handling Your Guinea Pig

Guinea pigs do not like to be lifted and held unless they are gradually taught to tolerate it. If your guinea pig has not been held very much in his life, it will require skill and patience to teach him to accept it.

Warning!

Never, *ever* lift a guinea pig by any of his limbs. This practice is dangerous and painful to the guinea pig. Also, be careful never to hold a guinea pig tightly by his midsection. A tight grip on this area of the body could result in internal injuries.

Since guinea pigs are not natural climbers, your pet will feel awkward and insecure when lifted off the ground. As a result, he may struggle frantically. A fall can seriously injure a guinea pig. For this reason, you must learn to hold your guinea pig properly and securely.

Before you begin practicing picking up and carrying your guinea pig, be sure to wear protective clothing.

Bare skin and unclipped guinea pig nails don't mix!

The best way to pick up a guinea pig is to place one hand underneath the animal so that his legs are on either side of your hand and then lift him using the other hand to hold up his rear. Holding the guinea pig against your chest in this manner helps him feel secure. If he begins to struggle during the handling process, bend down to your knees. This will keep him from falling too far if you lose your grip on him.

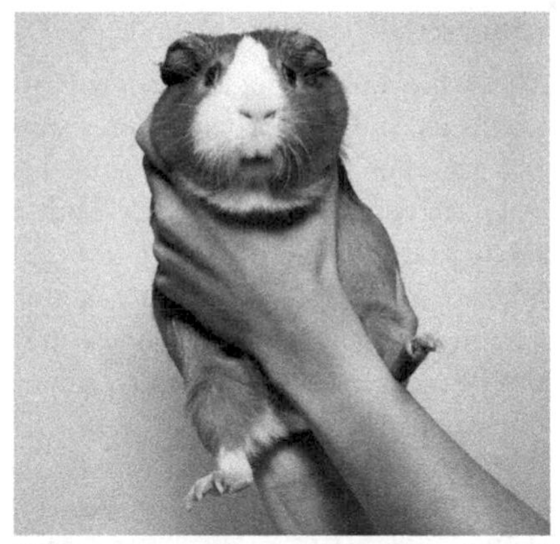

Lift a guinea pig with one hand under his chest and the other hand supporting his rump.

If you have children, keep a close eye on them when they wish to handle the guinea pig. Teach them the proper way to lift and carry a guinea pig, and always supervise them when they are doing so. Because guinea pigs are fragile and incorrect handling can result in a severely injured animal, very small children should not be permitted to pick up or carry a guinea pig. Petting a guinea pig while he has all four feet safely on the floor is a better approach when very young children are involved.

Remember when handling your guinea pig to always treat him gently and carefully. Since being lifted and carried is not natural for a guinea pig, you will need patience and kindness to help your new pet accept this type of handling.

Introducing Other Pets

Guinea pigs are very social animals and can get along with other pets, including cats, dogs, rabbits, and other guinea pigs. However, whether there is harmony in a particular multipet household depends largely on the individual animals involved, as well as the owner.

If your guinea pig is going to live happily in your home, he will need to get used to your other pets. It can take considerable time, patience, and commitment to teach your dog or cat to get along with a guinea pig. Never force pets on one another, and always supervise your animals while they are together. Make sure you devote special attention to this aspect of guinea pig ownership, since your guinea pig's life depends on it.

Guinea Pigs and Dogs

When it comes to dogs, guinea pig owners have to take special care. Dogs are predators, and guinea pigs are prey animals. It's instinctive for dogs to chase and kill guinea pigs, and it's instinctive for guinea pigs to fear dogs and run from them. If you are going to keep both a guinea pig and a dog, you need to be aware of this inherent tension between the two.

The safest way to handle a dog-guinea pig relationship is to never allow the dog and the guinea pig to be loose together in your home or backyard. No dog can be completely trusted with a small rodent like a guinea pig. A dog can kill a guinea pig in a few seconds.

Most dogs can be trained to respect a caged guinea pig, though. They can be taught not to harass the guinea pig while he is in his cage and to leave you alone while you are holding your guinea pig in your arms.

If you already have a dog and would like to bring a guinea pig into your home, there are some points you should consider. First of all, think about your dog's personality. Is she a mellow, old couch potato who is hard pressed to get upset or excited? Or is she a younger, more active dog? Dogs who are older and calmer usually do better when new pets are introduced. Be careful, though. The mellowest of dogs can suddenly come to life when she sees a guinea pig scurrying across the floor.

If you have a young, easily excitable dog, guinea pig ownership may still work out for you, provided you are able to control your dog. During the introduction process, you will have to be able to contain your dog's enthusiasm. If she ignores you when you call her and basically marches to the beat of her own drummer, you will have a problem.

Assuming your dog is controllable, think about her past relationships with other animals. Is she aggressive toward cats? Does she like to chase squirrels and other small animals? Have you encouraged her do this? If your answer to any of these questions is yes, you will have a difficult time teaching your dog that the new guinea pig is off-limits, since she has already learned that it's okay to chase smaller animals. You can certainly give it a try, but you may have to consider keeping the two animals apart forever or simply passing on guinea pig ownership.

Consider your dog's breed as well. Many terriers, some types of hounds, and a number of other breeds have been bred for hundreds of years to hunt small mammals. If your dog is of one of these hunting breeds, keep in mind that one look at your new guinea pig could trigger previously dormant hunting instincts in your dog. In this situation, you will have to work even harder to teach your dog to override her natural instincts and not harass your guinea pig.

If you have decided your dog is controlled enough to attempt making friends with a guinea pig, you can begin the gradual process of introducing the two animals. Make sure your new guinea pig has had some time to get used to his new home before you introduce him to your dog. Once he seems comfortable, start the proceedings by putting your dog on a leash and asking an adult whom the dog respects to control her.

Allow your dog to gradually approach the guinea pig's cage in a quiet manner. If the dog gets rambunctious, correct her by saying, "No!" and quickly pulling back on the leash. When the dog stands quietly, praise her to let her know that this is the kind of behavior you expect from her when she is close to the guinea pig.

When your guinea pig first lays eyes on your dog, he will most likely be frightened. He will probably dive into his nest box and hide. Let him stay there, because he will feel much more secure. Eventually, if the dog behaves in a nonthreatening manner, the guinea pig may become braver and more curious, finally venturing out of the nest box to investigate.

Once the dog and the guinea pig are comfortable with each other in this scenario and your guinea pig is used to being out of his cage without the dog present, you can try carrying your guinea pig in your arms with the dog present. Begin your session indoors by placing the dog on a leash. You may also want to muzzle her, just to be safe.

Take your guinea pig out of the cage and hold him in your arms as you move slowly across the room. Reassure the guinea pig with a soothing voice while the person holding the leash allows the dog to watch you. If the dog acts aggressively, correct her by saying, "No" and pulling back on the leash. If the dog sits by and quietly watches, praise her.

The guinea pig may become frightened by the dog's proximity and the fact that he is outside of his cage and may struggle to get away. Your dog's first impulse will be to get excited about this. Teach the dog that this is not acceptable, and don't allow her to run up and jump on you. Using the dog's obedience training, tell her to sit so she will come to understand that this is a special animal who cannot be harmed in any way. Repeat these exercises until your dog gets the message. (Muzzling your dog while the guinea pig is in your arms is highly recommended until you are completely confident that she will not harm the guinea pig.) It may take a couple of months, but if you are consistent, you should see results.

Regardless of how well your dog behaves with your guinea pig, *never leave the two alone together* loose in your home or yard. This is for your guinea pig's safety.

Guinea Pigs and Cats

Cats are usually better companions for guinea pigs than dogs, primarily because the two species are a bit closer in size. While cats are predators and may be inclined to chase guinea pigs, they are less capable of doing damage than a dog, who can kill a guinea pig with one snap of her jaws. It is rare that a cat will be so aggressive toward a guinea pig that the two cannot be housemates.

When preparing to introduce your cat and your guinea pig, start out by buying a harness for your cat and getting her used to wearing it. Having your cat in a harness during the introduction outside your guinea pig's cage will give you control over her should she become aggressive. You should also have a water pistol nearby in case your cat gets out of hand and you need to squirt her to discourage undesirable behavior.

Start out by showing the guinea pig to your cat while the guinea pig is still in his cage. The two animals will be very wary of each other at first, and the guinea pig may hide in his nest box. If your cat approaches tentatively and does not behave aggressively toward the guinea pig, reward her with praise and a treat. If she hisses at the guinea pig and runs away, ignore it. She will undoubtedly come

A cat can be a good companion for a guinea pig. However, you must closely supervise all interactions.

back to investigate and will eventually get used to the intruder. If the cat reaches her arm into the cage and tries to get at the guinea pig, squirt her rump with the water pistol from a distance. This will let her know that this kind of behavior toward the guinea pig reaps unpleasant results.

Once the two animals begin to ignore each other, you'll know you are ready for the next step. Allow your guinea pig out of his cage indoors, with your cat in the harness being held by another adult. When the guinea pig moves, the cat may act as if she wants to chase the guinea pig. Don't allow it. Instead, keep the cat still and let her watch the guinea pig move around the room until she gets used to the idea that she's not allowed to chase.

You will need to repeat these get-acquainted sessions often until both animals are comfortable with each other. It may take some time, but in most cases, your efforts will pay off.

Of course, the safest way to have a cat and a guinea pig in the same home is to keep the guinea pig caged or secure in your arms while the cat is present. *Never, under any circumstances*, leave your cat and guinea pig alone together unsupervised.

Other Guinea Pigs

Fostering cohabitation between two guinea pigs can be complicated. In the wild, guinea pigs live with their own kind in complex societies. Whenever a guinea pig is introduced to a member of his own species, the two rodents have to figure out just where each one of them fits in the pecking order.

The first step toward a successful friendship among guinea pigs is spaying and neutering, particularly in the case of two males. Raging hormones can cause an intact male guinea pig to fight with another guinea pig he might otherwise get along with. Spaying and neutering both female and male guinea pigs eliminates hormones from the equation, making the animals calmer and more docile.

When deciding whether two guinea pigs will become friends, keep in mind that gender can be an important factor. Spayed females and neutered males tend to get along better than other gender combinations, although two intact females have been known to become good friends.

Introducing two guinea pigs is different than introducing a dog and a guinea pig or a cat and a guinea pig. Guinea pigs see other guinea pigs differently than they do members of other species and are capable of behaving much more aggressively with each other. In many situations, guinea pigs who are strangers will seriously fight. This is why it is necessary to gradually allow them to get used to each other.

Most guinea pigs enjoy the company of other guinea pigs.

Begin by finding a neutral territory where neither guinea pig has had a chance to stake a claim. This can be a room in the house where neither has been, or even the backseat of a parked car. Placing the guinea pigs on unclaimed turf will temper their instinctive urge to defend their own territory. Keep the guinea pigs in their individual cages at first, and put the cages next to each other on neutral turf. Leave them together like this as often as possible.

Once their tensions have subsided and they seem less hostile toward each other through the bars of their cages, take them out and let them get close to each other, still in the neutral place. There might be some fighting, but you can break it up by squirting a water pistol at the two culprits. Provided you have not mixed two intact males, the guinea pigs will eventually work things out and will learn to tolerate each other or, hopefully, become fast friends. Again, this is much more likely if the guinea pigs are spayed or neutered.

Keep in mind that placing intact male and female guinea pigs together will soon result in numerous litters of baby guinea pigs. Since there are already more guinea pigs than there are homes for them, the most responsible thing to do is avoid keeping intact males and females together. This problem of reproduction can be solved, of course, by having the animals spayed or neutered.

Litter Box Training

The guinea pig's denning instinct makes him a candidate for litter box training; guinea pigs, just like cats and rabbits, prefer not to foul the area where they eat and sleep. Some guinea pigs can be trained to use a litter box, although they are not as good at it as rabbits. If you would like to try litter box training your guinea pig, have patience and accept the fact that your pet may never be 100 percent reliable.

The most important things to remember when litter box training a guinea pig are consistency and praise. Never scold your guinea pig for not using the litter box since this will only frighten and confuse him. Another important point is to work gradually, starting out your guinea pig in a small space and, hopefully, expanding to more and more rooms of the whole house.

Most guinea pig owners use organic cat litter for their guinea pig's litter box, especially brands made from corn, paper, wheat, or grass. Stay away from clay- and wood-based litters, since these tend to be dusty and can cause respiratory problems for guinea pigs. Some pet supply stores specializing in small mammals

Your guinea pig will appreciate you keeping his environment clean.

Cleaning Up

While your guinea pig is learning to use the litter box, clean up after him by picking up fecal pellets with a tissue and washing urine marks on carpeting with a mixture of vinegar and water. Urine on wood floors can be cleaned with soap and water.

Pick up any solid matter from your guinea pig's litter box every day, and once or twice a week empty the box entirely, clean it with a water and vinegar solution, and dry it thoroughly before filling it with litter and returning it to its usual spot.

will carry litter made just for them. This is the best type to buy. You can also use straw on top of a layer of newspaper as litter, although it will be less absorbent than most commercially made brands.

Start Small

Start the litter box training process in a very small area, preferably the guinea pig's cage. Place a small litter box (a plastic washing-up bin with low sides that's big enough for him to stand in comfortably) in a corner of your pet's cage, attached to the side with a clip or twistable wire so you can remove it for cleaning. Try to place the box in the area of the cage that your guinea pig tends to use as a bathroom and far away from his food, water, and nest box. Put some fecal pellets in the box to help give him the right idea and then add a handful of hay to a corner of the box to encourage your guinea pig to use it.

Try to keep an eye on your guinea pig while he is in his cage. When you see him defecate in the litter box, offer him a treat as a reward (see chapter 6 for suitable treats). Don't be alarmed if the guinea pig sits in the box and munches on the hay you've placed in it, since guinea pigs will often eat and defecate at the same time. Munching on the hay will stimulate your guinea pig's digestive system and may cause him to use the box, as you intended.

If your guinea pig prefers to sleep in his litter box rather than use it as a toilet, you may want to provide him with a more attractive bed than the one he has. Try using a different bedding material.

Once your guinea pig seems to be using the litter box in his cage and has been allowed to do so for some time, you can try giving him a little more space.

Create a special part of the house just for him. (Kitchens, bathrooms, or hallways work best.) Use a baby gate to section off a small area so you can still keep an eye on him.

Place the litter box in the small area, along with the guinea pig's food, water, and bedding. Watch your guinea pig to make sure he uses the litter box regularly. If he is using the litter box successfully, you can increase the amount of space in the house that is accessible to him.

If your guinea pig starts making mistakes at any point in the process, it may have been too soon to place him in a bigger area. Return him to his cage and start over. Or you may want to try buying a few more litter boxes and placing them in various parts of the guinea pig's space. With many litter box options to choose from, he is more likely to get the right idea.

Remember that your guinea pig may never learn to use the litter box reliably and will more than likely have occasional accidents. Patience, understanding, and a sense of humor will help you cope with this situation. Try to come up with ideas of how to adapt to your guinea pig's bathroom habits.

Chapter 6

Feeding Your Guinea Pig

The way you feed your guinea pig can mean the difference between a healthy, long-lived pet and a sickly, unhappy animal. Guinea pigs are herbivores, and in the wild they are browsers—animals who spend considerable amounts of time foraging for and eating plants. Because plant material is difficult to break down, the digestive tract of the guinea pig is quite different from that of carnivores (like cats) and omnivores (like us).

It's important to give your guinea pig a diet that simulates the diet she would eat in the wild. Failure to do so will result in a guinea pig with chronic diarrhea; heart, liver, and kidney disease; and obesity.

Pellets

People usually think of pelleted foods as something only rabbits eat, but specially made pellets just for guinea pigs are the mainstay of a healthy guinea pig's diet. When supplemented with fresh foods, these pellets provide balanced nutrition for the guinea pig.

Guinea pigs, unlike most other mammals, are unable to manufacture vitamin C within their bodies and also need a lot of folic acid, so it's important to feed them pellets made especially for guinea pigs because these pellets contain those nutrients. When you buy a pelleted guinea pig food, look for a product that contains at least 8 percent protein, 16 percent fiber, and 1 gram of vitamin C per kilogram. Read the packaging to be sure the pellets are labeled as nutritionally complete.

Avoid foods that contain animal products, beet pulp, corn products, seeds, nuts, oils, vegetable fiber, rice bran, and rice flour. Additives such as corn syrup, sucrose, propylene glycol, food colorings, propyl gallate, potassium sorbate, sodium nitrate, sodium nitrite, sodium metabisulfate, ethoxyquin, and butylated hydroxyanisole should also be avoided.

Do not buy a large supply of pellets, since they will lose their nutritional value over time. Get just as much as your guinea pig will eat in about a month. Store the food in the refrigerator, where it will stay fresher longer.

If your guinea pig is younger than 3 months old, you may leave a bowl of pellets in her cage at all times to eat whenever she wishes. However, if you have an adult, you should provide two servings of two tablespoons each day. Feeding the animal once in the morning and once in the evening is ideal. If the guinea pig starts to become obese, you may have to cut back to one tablespoon per day. You may also want to try increasing her exercise time.

If your guinea pig does not eat all the pellets you place in her dish, throw the old ones away before you refill the bowl. It's important to offer only fresh pellets.

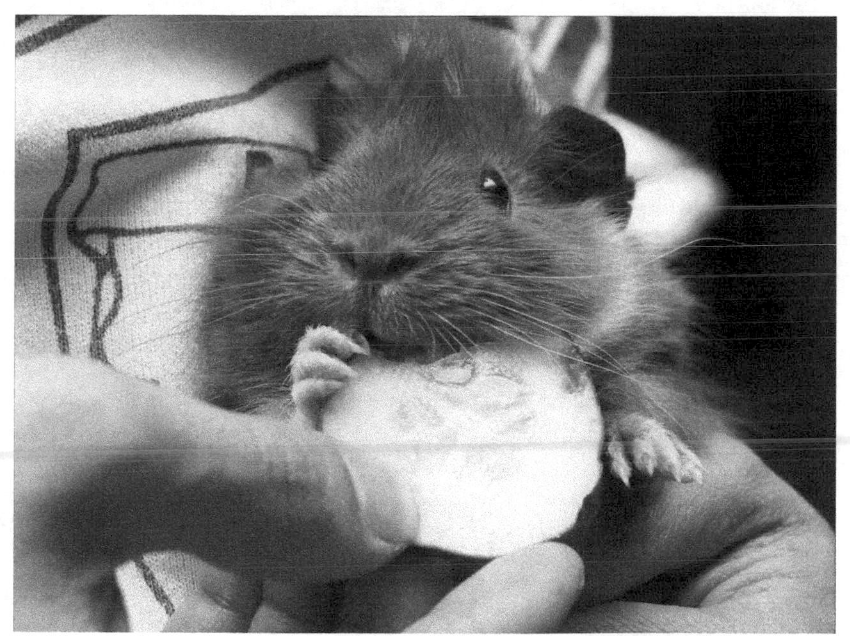

Pellets are the mainstay of a guinea pig's diet, but she will also need fresh foods.

Feeding Tips

- Wash your guinea pig's food dish every day to prevent bacteria buildup.
- Feed your pet pellets formulated especially for guinea pigs as a dietary staple.
- Offer a variety of fresh greens daily.
- Stick to a regular feeding schedule for your guinea pig. Once in the morning and once in the evening is ideal.
- Make sure your guinea pig has ample access to fresh hay.
- Keep a water bottle filled with fresh water at all times. Check it frequently, especially in the summer, to make sure there is an ample supply.

Hay

When you bought your guinea pig's cage or hutch, you also bought a hay rack. Guinea pigs need free access to fibrous foods, and hay, which is pure roughage, fits the bill.

Hay can be obtained from a number of sources, including pet supply stores, feed stores, and local horse stables. When you buy hay, check it for freshness. Good, clean hay should have a sweet smell and minimal dust. Examine it for mold, which can be very harmful to guinea pigs if ingested. Do not buy hay that is wet or damp. When you get it home, store the hay in a cool place protected from rain or dampness.

You'll find different types of hay to choose from. Your pet supply store will stock packaged alfalfa and timothy hay, while feed stores and stables will have baled hay. Timothy hay is generally the best. If your guinea pig is eating pellets, alfalfa hay is already included in her diet. The addition of more alfalfa may cause her to become overweight. (Hay cubes, manufactured for horses, are not recommended for guinea pigs.)

Your guinea pig needs fresh hay every day to keep her digestive system healthy.

Give your guinea pig a handful of fresh hay every day to keep her digestive system in working order. Place the hay in the hay rack to help keep it from scattering around the cage. Remove old hay from the cage and the rack before you replace it with new hay.

Greens

Pellets and hay are not the only foods your guinea pig needs. Fresh greens are also an important part of her diet and should be provided daily. Some of the best fresh foods for guinea pigs include dark green vegetables such as romaine lettuce, dandelion greens, carrot tops, broccoli, basil, spinach, and artichokes. Many other leafy green vegetables that humans eat are good for guinea pigs, too, provided the leaves are dark green. Dark green leaves provide your guinea pig with valuable vitamin C, which she cannot manufacture on her own.

Growing a Guinea Pig Garden

You may want to consider growing a garden for your guinea pig, where she can forage for greens as nature intended. Good garden plants that are healthy for guinea pigs include coltsfoot, dandelions, dead nettles, ground elder, mugwort, plantain, ragwort, shepherd's purse, and yarrow. Guinea pigs also like to nibble on Bermuda grass and clover.

To create a guinea pig garden, set aside a patch of your backyard just for your pet's plants. Be sure to use organic soil and no pesticides or chemical fertilizers. When the plants are mature, create a protective enclosure for your guinea pig. Then let your guinea pig run loose among the plants to graze to her heart's content. As you supervise her, you'll have the opportunity to see your guinea pig's wild side as she indulges her natural browsing instincts. (There are many common plants that are poisonous, so your pet's foraging should be restricted to plants that are known to be safe. That includes weeding her garden *before* you turn her loose.)

If your guinea pig never goes outside, you can grow some of these same plants in a large tray on your balcony or fire escape, bring the tray inside every so often, and let your guinea pig munch on them. She will enjoy the opportunity to harvest her own greens and you will have fun observing her.

Let your guinea pig visit the garden or tray once or twice a week. On the other days, be sure to provide her with different greens than the ones you are growing, so she will have variety in her diet.

If your guinea pig is not used to eating fresh foods, introduce these items gradually to her diet so she does not get diarrhea. Start by offering her one new food item once a week. Eventually your guinea pig should be receiving three different types of fresh greens daily, making up no more than 15 percent of her diet. Remember to promptly remove uneaten greens from your guinea pig's cage.

You may find that your guinea pig has a sensitivity to a particular vegetable. You'll know because she will get diarrhea not long after she eats it. If this happens, remove the offending food from her diet.

Dark, leafy greens give your pet the vitamin C she needs.

Make sure the greens you offer your guinea pig are fresh. Buy them from the produce department of your supermarket, from a health food store, or from a farm stand, and be sure to wash them thoroughly. Do not gather greens from fields unless you can be completely certain the plants have not been sprayed with chemicals and that they are not poisonous. Organically grown greens, if you can find them, are by far the best choice for guinea pigs.

Treats

Guinea pigs enjoy receiving occasional treats. Feeding her treats will help the two of you bond and will supplement her diet. The healthiest treats to feed your guinea pig are fresh fruits. Some that guinea pigs enjoy include oranges, apples, pears, strawberries, peaches, melons, and tomatoes. While these items are particularly popular among guinea pigs, you can offer your pet just about any

Fresh fruits are the healthiest treats to give your guinea pig.

fruit. Just be sure to feed in moderation. (Carrots, though not a fruit, are also a guinea pig favorite.)

Commercially prepared treats can also be acceptable for guinea pigs, as long as you don't overfeed. Avoid giving your guinea pig commercial treats that contain sugar or dairy products. It's also wise to refrain from offering your pet traditional human treats that are high in sugar or salt, including candy and chocolate.

Occasionally, you may also want to give your guinea pig some dried and aged twigs from an unsprayed fruit tree as a treat. Guinea pigs love to gnaw on branches and sometimes rip off the bark and eat it. (Drying and aging is important since some tree branches are poisonous when fresh.)

Cecotropes

Several decades ago, researchers discovered that some small mammals have an unusual way of supplementing their diets. Small, soft pellets known as cecotropes are produced by the guinea pig's cecum (a part of the large intestine).

Supplements

In addition to providing leafy greens for your guinea pig, you can also supplement her vitamin C intake by adding 100 milligrams of ascorbic acid in the form of a syrup or a tablet (the kind made for humans works well) in each cup of drinking water that you give your guinea pig.

While many pet supply stores stock mineral licks intended for small mammals, most guinea pigs do not need a mineral block if they are on a diet that includes pellets. Nutritionally complete pellets made for guinea pigs include enough minerals.

These cecotropes, which contain special nutrients, pass from the anus and are then instinctively eaten by the guinea pig. While this may seem very strange to us, nature developed this system to help the guinea pig absorb nutrients from the hard-to-digest cellulose material contained in plants.

For your guinea pig to get the most nutrition from her vegetarian diet, she must be able to consume an adequate amount of the cecotropes produced by her body. Since these pellets are usually ingested just as they leave the anus, you may occasionally see your guinea pig eating them as they are produced. Do not discourage her from doing this. She knows the difference between these pellets and her waste materials.

Water

Water is very important to the guinea pig, as it is to any living creature, and should be provided at all times. Change your guinea pig's water daily and wash the water bottle out regularly. Be sure to keep a close eye on the water level in your guinea pig's bottle in the summer or whenever she is exposed to heat.

Chapter 7

Grooming Your Guinea Pig

One of the first things you'll notice when you start living with a guinea pig is that he loves to groom himself. Guinea pigs are much like cats in that respect—always preening and primping. Even though your guinea pig grooms himself, he will also appreciate regular grooming from you. Grooming can help you both bond and will also provide you with a chance to look your guinea pig over for any signs of health problems.

It's best to set aside one hour a week for grooming your shorthaired guinea pig. (Longhaired breeds must be groomed every day.) Guinea pigs tend to shed more at certain times of the year, and during these shedding seasons, it is best to brush your pet at least every other day. In the early fall, hair begins to fall out in larger quantities than normal. In the winter, the shed hairs are replaced by more fur that will help keep the animal warm. When you are ready, gather your grooming tools and find a comfortable spot where you can sit with your guinea pig on your lap. While you are preparing to brush him is a good time to check his eyes and ears for discharge and examine the bottoms of his feet for sores.

Your Guinea Pig's Grooming Tools

To groom your guinea pig, you'll need a brush, a comb, and a nail trimmer. A slicker or pin brush is best for brushing guinea pigs' fur. This type of brush is gentle yet effective at removing snarls and mats. If your guinea pig is a shorthaired breed, a flea comb (the type used for cats) is another good grooming tool. If your guinea pig is a longhaired variety, you'll need a wide-tooth comb rather than a fine-tooth flea comb.

Since a guinea pig's toenails need to be trimmed regularly, make sure you have a nail trimmer. The guillotine type used for cutting cats' claws will work, although many guinea pig owners prefer to use human nail clippers instead.

Brushing and Combing

Begin your grooming session by brushing your guinea pig. You will notice a lot of loose hairs are coming out. Since guinea pigs tend to shed at any time of year, this is normal. Use the comb to smooth and finish after brushing and for sensitive areas such as around the face, ears, tummy, and legs.

When you are brushing and combing your pet, keep an eye out for parasites such as lice and mites. Lice are small, flattened insects, and their presence is usually accompanied by itching, scratching, and hair loss. Mites are microscopic but also cause itching, hair loss, and scabby skin. If you suspect there may be lice or mites on your pet, contact your veterinarian. They can provide you with safe medications designed to kill lice and mites and give you details on how to eliminate these parasites from your guinea pig's environment. *Never* use any product made for treating dogs or cats, as these are far too toxic for guinea pigs.

As you brush or comb your guinea pig, keep an eye out for any lumps or sores on the animal's body that could be an indication of disease or infection.

A longhaired guinea pig will need more frequent brushing.

If your guinea pig has long hair, you will need to use your brush to work out any mats you may find in his coat. Pay particular attention to areas where one part of the body rubs against another, such as the armpits and groin. Regular, careful grooming will prevent mats from forming. Another option for longhaired guinea pigs is to have them trimmed by a professional groomer who is experienced in handling guinea pigs.

Trimming Toenails

Trimming your guinea pig's toenails is a necessary part of your grooming sessions, although it will not need to be done every week. Check the length and condition of your guinea pig's nails every time you groom him. When the nails appear to be getting long, it is time to trim them.

Prepare to trim your guinea pig's nails by placing him gently in your lap with his legs facing upward. Use your clipper to take off a small portion of the nail. Be careful not to cut the quick (the pink part running inside the center of the nail); doing so can cause pain to the guinea pig and a bloody toenail. A silhouette of the quick can be seen by holding the nail up to the light.

If you are nervous about trimming your guinea pig's nails for the first time, or if your guinea pig struggles when you try to hold him in your lap, you may want to ask your veterinarian to show you how to perform this necessary function.

Bathing

Although you might be tempted at times, try to avoid giving your guinea pig a bath. As a rule, guinea pigs don't enjoy being bathed and rarely need to be, unless they are show animals. If your guinea pig needs his bottom cleaned, try to cleanse it with mild soap and water without submerging the entire guinea pig in water. Once you have finished, make sure the guinea pig is completely dry before you put him back in his cage, since a wet bottom and feet can attract egg-laying flies on outdoor guinea pigs or result in sores on the skin.

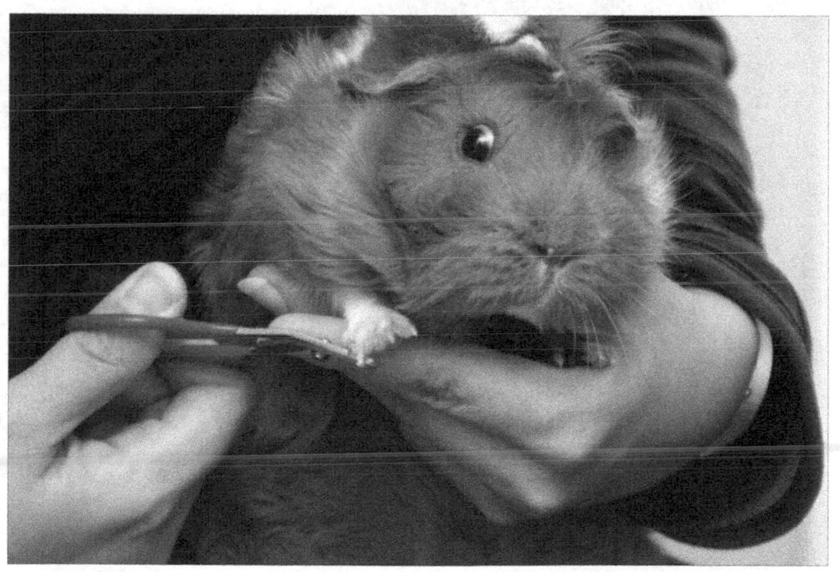

Regular nail trimming is an essential part of your pet's care.

A bath and a minor trim with scissors every few months might be in order if you have a longhaired breed such as a Peruvian, Silky, or Texel. You must comb your longhaired pet out carefully before the bath because any mats or tangles will become like lumps of cement once they are wet.

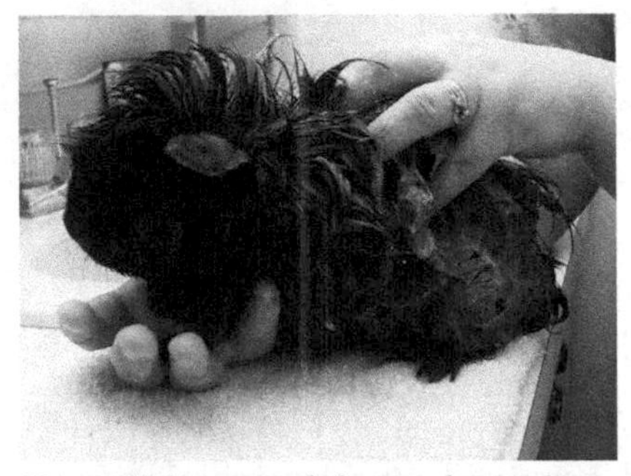

Use a mild shampoo made for cats—human shampoos will dry your pet's coat.

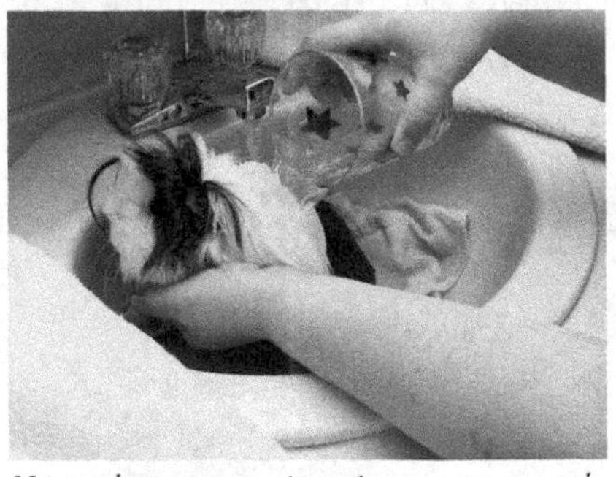

Never submerge your guinea pig; use a cup to gently wet him.

Use a mild shampoo designed for dogs or cats when bathing your pet, and be sure to use lukewarm water. Keep the water in the sink shallow, and use a cup to gently pour water on your guinea pig to wet his fur. Be sure to rinse the soap thoroughly out of his coat. Take care not to get water in your cavy's ears or eyes.

When it's time to dry your cavy, put him in a warm, draft-free area. Cuddle him with a towel. You can also blow-dry your cavy using your hair dryer on a *low* setting. Take care not to burn him with the hair dryer, and don't force the issue. The noise and rushing air might frighten him. Just keep him warm and safe until he dries naturally.

Chapter 8

Keeping Your Guinea Pig Healthy

Guinea pigs who are well fed and properly cared for rarely get sick. However, if a guinea pig's basic needs, including a proper diet, a clean environment, and regular bonding and exercise, are not met, the animal becomes susceptible to a number of dangerous illnesses. In other words, taking good care of your guinea pig will result in a healthy pet. And, since many guinea pig ailments are difficult to cure, prevention is the best policy.

Guinea Pig Anatomy

The body of the guinea pig is the result of her wild ancestors' evolution and adaptations. Her anatomy is designed to help her carry out her most important tasks: eating, reproducing, and fleeing from predators.

The guinea pig has a short, stocky body, no tail, and large eyes. The front feet are flat and usually have four digits with claws. The hind feet have three digits with claws and are much longer than the front feet. Full-grown domestic guinea pigs weigh between two and three pounds and measure about ten inches long.

The Coat

The domestic guinea pig comes in a variety of colors (see chapter 3), thanks to selective breeding by humans. Natural selection played no part in the varied patterns of the domestic guinea pig, with the exception of one: agouti. Agouti

Your guinea pig's coat is made up of long guard hairs and a fine undercoat.

is the color pattern nature gave the guinea pig to help conceal her in the wild. Regardless of color, all guinea pigs' coats are made up of large, coarse guard hairs and an undercoat of finer hair. Each hair on the guinea pig's body has a follicle, which is located near a sebaceous gland. The guinea pig's sebaceous glands provide oil to the skin and coat to keep it healthy.

The guinea pig's entire body is covered with hair, except for her ear flaps, the area just behind the ear, and the pads of her feet. Five or six rows of whiskers are located on each side of the guinea pig's nose.

Bones and Muscles

The guinea pig's skeleton and muscular structure give the animal speed for quick getaways and the ability to efficiently eat plants—her natural diet. The thirty-four vertebrae and thirteen to fourteen ribs provide the primary frame of the guinea pig's body. This frame supports a relatively large skull, which makes up about one-third of the guinea pig's total body weight.

The muscles that cover the skeleton are called skeletal muscles. These muscles are what enable the guinea pig to move rapidly and do all the other physical activities typical of guinea pigs.

The most impressive muscles on the guinea pig's body are the masticatory muscles, located on the jaw. These muscles enable the guinea pig to gnaw on husks, pods, and shells to get to the seeds inside and to grind this tough food down into fine particles. These are necessary requirements for an animal whose entire diet consists of plant material.

The guinea pig's dentition—twenty teeth in all—is very important to her survival. She has chisel-like incisors and rootless molars. All these teeth continue to grow throughout the animal's life to compensate for the fact that they wear down through constant use.

Digestive System

The guinea pig's gastrointestinal system is designed to efficiently digest plant fiber and is able to turn 80 percent of the food she eats into energy. The process begins with the softening of the food in the animal's stomach, from where it moves down into the large intestine. From there, what has not yet been digested goes to a part of the guinea pig's anatomy called the cecum. Similar to a human appendix, the cecum is on the left side of the guinea pig's body and makes up about 15 percent of the animal's entire weight. The cecum's function is to house bacteria that can break down the cellulose in plant matter. This cellulose is turned into carbohydrate constituents, which are digestible.

Before the guinea pig can obtain the nutrients from the plant matter digested in the cecum, the food material must return to the stomach. This is achieved through a process called refection. The guinea pig expels the material in pellet form from her anus and then eats it. Once the pellet gets to the stomach, the carbohydrates are absorbed.

Guinea Pig Teeth

Like all rodents, your guinea pig's teeth are constantly growing. She needs to chew on something hard, such as a block of untreated wood, to keep the teeth properly worn down.

If a guinea pig's teeth are misaligned and she can't wear them down properly, the condition is called malocclusion. If you notice that your guinea pig's teeth don't fit together properly (the top teeth should overlap the lower), take her to the vet, who will properly recommend regular trimming of the teeth or their removal.

Reproduction

Guinea pigs are known for their ability to reproduce quickly and prolifically. This is one of the reasons for their popularity as a food animal in many South American cultures.

The female guinea pig becomes able to breed at the age of 4 weeks, although the healthiest young are produced when she has reached at least 12 weeks of age. Males are ready to breed when they are 8 to 9 weeks old.

Females go into heat every thirteen to twenty-one days. Babies are born anywhere from fifty-six to seventy-four days after breeding. Litters usually range from one to thirteen babies, but four is most typical. The female guinea pig has only two teats with which to nurse her young, so many of the babies born in very large litters often do not survive.

The young are born with furry bodies and with their eyes open and are able to eat solid food within a day after being born. They are weaned within three weeks to a month after birth, making them self-sufficient creatures at an early age.

Find a Veterinarian

Many people think only cats and dogs need to go to a veterinarian. This is not true. Small mammals such as guinea pigs also deserve veterinary treatment if they become ill or injured.

Since your guinea pig's body differs considerably from that of a cat or dog, some of the treatments and medications appropriate for these other pets could be harmful to your guinea pig. In fact, certain antibiotics commonly given to other small animals can kill a guinea pig. Given this, it's important to only use a vet who has experience in treating guinea pigs.

No matter what kind of pet you own, it's best not to wait until you have an emergency to go looking for a veterinarian. Since vets who specialize in treating guinea pigs are harder to find, it is wise to select your guinea pig's veterinarian before she actually needs one.

The best way to find a guinea pig vet is by referral. Ask other guinea pig owners who they use and whether they are happy with that individual or clinic. Speak to the breeder or rescuer from whom you got your guinea pig. If you don't know any other guinea pig owners, contact the House Rabbit Society (see the appendix). They can help you locate a guinea pig veterinarian in your area. Or call your local county extension office and get the name and number of the guinea pig 4-H project leader in your area. They should be able to refer you to a veterinarian who treats guinea pigs.

Look for a veterinarian who has some experience in treating guinea pigs.

Once you have selected a veterinarian, you may want to take your new guinea pig in for an examination. The vet will be able to tell you if your pet has any potential health problems and will set up an appointment for a spay or neuter if you wish to have this surgery performed. This meeting will also give you an opportunity to get to know the vet and give them the chance to start a file on your pet. This may also be a good time to ask your vet to show you how to clip your guinea pig's nails and answer any questions you may have on how to care for your new pet.

Observation

Get to know your guinea pig and keep a close eye on her. If you know how she looks when she is healthy, you'll be more likely to recognize signs of illness early on. Many diseases that can be fatal are curable in their earliest stages. Realizing your guinea pig is under the weather before she becomes seriously ill could mean the difference between life and death.

Regular grooming is an important part of observation, since this hands-on procedure will encourage you to take a close look at your pet. The tasks required

Signs of Poor Health

How will you know if your guinea pig isn't feeling well? In addition to drastic changes in behavior, look for these telltale signs:

- A dull look in the eyes
- Lethargy
- Loss of appetite
- Constipation or diarrhea
- Discharge from the eyes or nose
- Bloated abdomen
- Labored breathing
- Unexplained weight loss

If your guinea pig exhibits any of these signs, contact your veterinarian immediately.

of regular grooming, such as maintaining your pet's nails and brushing, will help you prevent serious illness and injury.

Examine your guinea pig's cage floor or litter box regularly. Keep an eye out for diarrhea or lack of feces, both of which can indicate a problem.

Preventing Disease

If you follow the feeding and housing guidelines in this book, your guinea pig should live a long and healthy life. However, you can also take extra precautions to ward off illness and deal with problems effectively, should they come up.

Diet

Probably the single most important step you can take to make sure your guinea pig stays healthy is to feed her a proper diet. Your guinea pig needs to eat certain foods to ensure all her body systems work properly. (See chapter 6 for complete information on your pet's nutritional requirements.) A correctly functioning system will help your guinea pig ward off a number of afflictions that often trouble less well-fed animals.

When changing your guinea pig's diet or adding a new food, remember to always do so gradually, slowly adding the new food in small amounts over time. A sudden alteration of what your pet is eating can wreak havoc on her digestive system and cause her to become seriously ill.

An extremely important element in your guinea pig's diet is water. Your guinea pig should always have access to clean, fresh water to keep her body functioning properly. Lack of water can result in a number of life-threatening conditions in guinea pigs.

Cleanliness

Another vitally important factor in keeping your guinea pig healthy is cleanliness. An unsanitary cage is a breeding ground for disease. A number of illnesses can be directly traced to dirty floors and nest boxes and unclean food bowls and water bottles. Every day, remove fouled bedding and fecal matter, and scrub your guinea pig's food dish and water bottle. Wash your pet's cage or hutch once a week to keep bacteria at a minimum.

The most important thing you can do for you pet's health is to feed her a good diet.

Stress can be extremely harmful to a guinea pig.

Stress

Like humans, guinea pigs are susceptible to stress. But unlike most humans, your guinea pig cannot do much to change her life and alleviate the stress. She relies on you to do it for her.

Stress has serious consequences for the body's immune system. You may have noticed that when you are under a lot of stress, you tend to catch colds more easily. The same is true for guinea pigs, although the ailments they catch can be much more dangerous than the common cold.

Do your best to keep your guinea pig's stress to a minimum. This means the animal should not be exposed to loud noises, excessive handling, severe temperature changes, or situations that will frighten her. Guinea pigs also need regular exercise and companionship, and providing these will reduce the amount of stress in your pet's life. Keeping stress to a minimum will result in a guinea pig with a healthy immune system that is able to fight off the various bacteria, fungus, and parasites to which she may be exposed.

Common Ailments

There are quite a few illnesses that affect a guinea pig, but many are rarely seen. What follows is a list of the most common health problems in pet guinea pigs today.

Abscesses

Abscesses are bacterial infections that result from a puncture wound of some kind. If your guinea pig has cut herself on something or has had a fight with another pet, she may develop an abscess at the site of the injury. You will recognize an abscess by its round appearance, usually accompanied by a pus discharge. Your veterinarian will need to treat your guinea pig with antibiotics to help her fight off the infection.

Anal Impaction

Older, unneutured male guinea pigs sometimes suffer from a condition known as anal impaction. (Females and younger, neutered males can also develop this problem, although it is not common.) This condition is caused by a weakness in the muscles of the anus, making it difficult for the cavy to pass fecal and cecael pellets. Cavies with this problem have a hard lump around the rectal area, are producing little or no feces, and begin to lose condition over time. If you suspect this problem in your guinea pig, take him to a veterinarian.

Bladder Stones

Some guinea pigs have a propensity to develop stones in their bladder. The signs of this problem include blood in the urine and squeaking while urinating and defecating. If left untreated, bladder stones can result in death. If you see signs of this condition in your guinea pig, seek veterinary care immediately.

Constipation/Diarrhea

Difficulty in defecating (constipation) or very loose stools (diarrhea) can be the result of poor diet or an illness (too many greens are a common cause of diarrhea). Symptoms of constipation are straining to defecate, lack of feces,

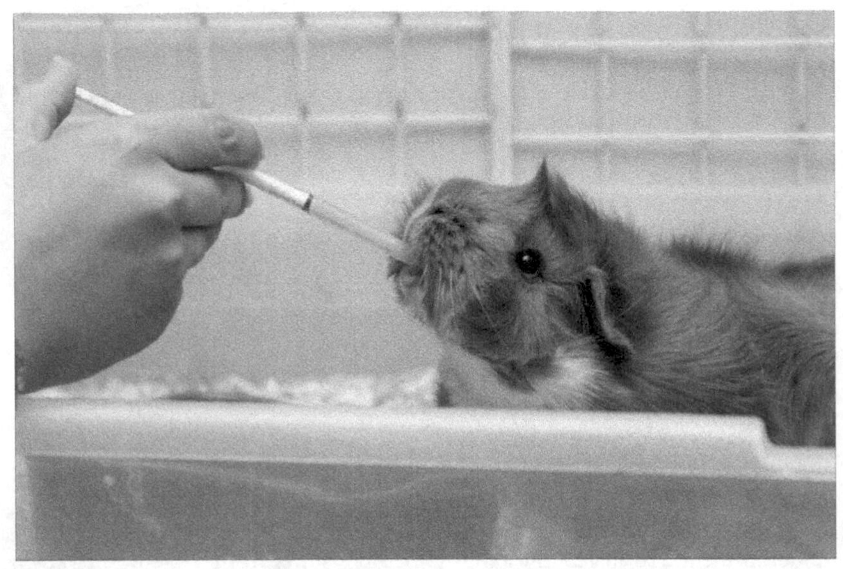

Be sure to follow your veterinarian's instructions for treating any health problem in your pet.

distended abdomen, and lethargy. Diarrhea is usually detected by loose or runny stools and a dirty bottom. Your veterinarian will need to determine what is causing the problem in either case, so it can be treated.

Flies

Flies can be dangerous to outdoor guinea pigs. They often lay their eggs on a guinea pig's soiled rectal area, leaving maggots to burrow into the skin and feed on the animal's flesh. Flies can be kept at bay by ensuring that both your guinea pig's cage and her fur are kept clean. If flies do lay eggs on your guinea pig, contact a veterinarian for assistance.

Heat Prostration

Guinea pigs are very susceptible to overheating. When the weather is hot, keep a close eye on your pet. Signs of heat prostration include a stretched out posture, panting, rapid breathing, and slobbering. If you find your guinea pig in this state, move her to a cool place out of the sun and put a cold, wet towel around her body, or bathe her in cool water. Heat prostration is an emergency situation. Contact your veterinarian immediately.

Lice

Lice are a common problem for guinea pigs. These tiny, wingless insects live in the hair of infested guinea pigs. Many pet guinea pigs suffer from light infestations of lice that is not obvious to their owners. If the infestation becomes heavy, however, the guinea pig will begin to scratch and lose hair, and scabs may form on the skin. If you suspect your guinea pig has lice, take her to a veterinarian for diagnosis. Since guinea pig lice are easily spread to other guinea pigs (but not to people), it is best to keep your healthy pet from associating with other members of her species who may be contaminated.

Malocclusion

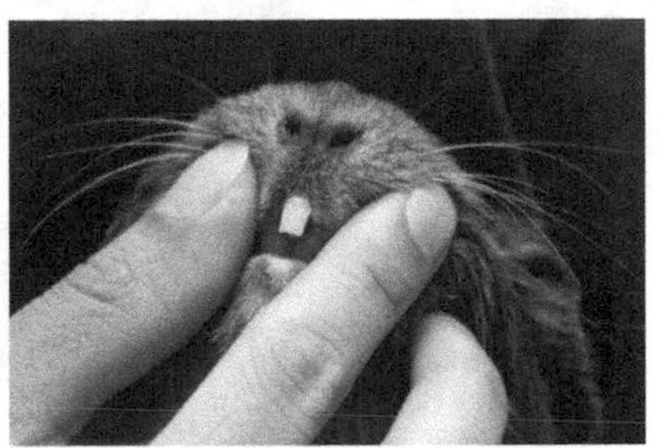

These teeth are correctly aligned. Misaligned teeth are a serious problem for guinea pigs and will need special attention throughout your pet's life.

When a guinea pig's front teeth do not wear down properly, the condition is known as malocclusion. This problem is usually the result of teeth that are misaligned and is genetic. Signs of malocclusion include overly long teeth, infections in the mouth, ulcerations on the lips or tongue, and difficulty eating. This is a common problem in guinea pigs and must be handled by a veterinarian or the guinea pig will eventually die. Treatment consists of a regular trimming of the teeth or their complete removal.

Mites

Guinea pigs are susceptible to a specific mite called *Trixacarus cavie.* This mite causes the guinea pig to lose patches of hair where the skin becomes red and scabby. Severely infested guinea pigs will run around wildly and in circles. Trixacarus mites are easily spread from one animal to another. Contact your veterinarian for help in treating this parasite.

Obesity

Veterinarians say obesity is a major health problem in guinea pigs. Guinea pigs who are overweight are prone to a number of illnesses affecting their major organs. The primary cause of obesity in guinea pigs is overfeeding pellets. Guinea pigs who are obese should be placed on a special diet to help them get down to their proper weight. If you are feeding your guinea pig too many pel-

Nutmeg is round and solid, as a guinea pig should be. But overfeeding leads to obesity, which poses serious health risks.

lets, cut back to the amount recommended for overweight cavies in chapter 6. If this does not result in a noticeable change in weight in a month or so, consult your veterinarian for help.

Respiratory Infections

Guinea pigs are prone to a number of viruses and bacteria that can cause respiratory infections. Symptoms include sneezing, discharge from the nose and eyes, loss of appetite, lethargy, and difficulty breathing. Prompt attention by a veterinarian is essential when a respiratory ailment is suspected.

Scurvy

Because guinea pigs cannot manufacture their own vitamin C (as many other mammals can), they are prone to scurvy, a disease caused by a deficiency in vitamin C. A guinea pig suffering from scurvy will have a poor appetite and swollen, painful joints and chest. She will be reluctant to move and/or will bleed from the gums. If scurvy is untreated, it can be fatal. A guinea pig with these symptoms should be taken to a veterinarian immediately.

Sore Hocks

Guinea pigs who live in a cage or hutch with a wire floor often develop sore hocks. This condition is typified by red, swollen skin on the hind legs, with accompanying hair loss. The guinea pig may also be reluctant to move. A veterinarian will provide an antibiotic ointment for treatment, along with a recommendation for a change in flooring.

Worms

Roundworms and tapeworms, two parasites that commonly afflict dogs and cats, also prey on guinea pigs. Symptoms of worm infestation include a distended abdomen, poor coat condition, and worms in the feces or near the anus. If you suspect your guinea pig has worms, contact your veterinarian. *Do not* use an over-the-counter wormer intended for dogs or cats as this can kill your guinea pig.

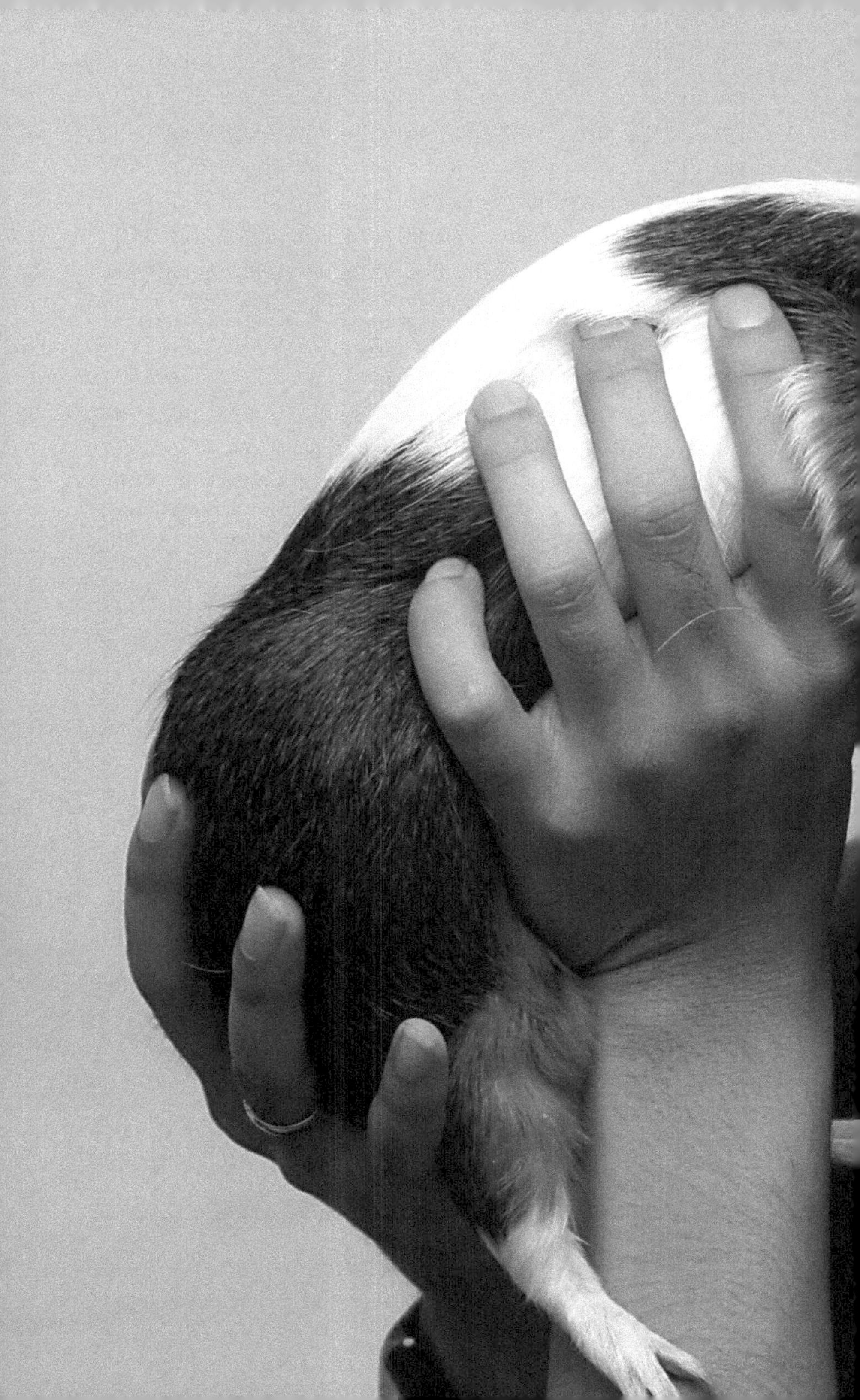

Part III

Enjoying Your Guinea Pig

Chapter 9

Your Guinea Pig's Behavior

To make your relationship with your guinea pig more rewarding, it's important to understand his behavior. Your pet guinea pig has not changed much since his species was domesticated thousands of years ago. The same instincts present in his ancestors live on in his genes. The domestic guinea pig is very similar to the wild cavy in the way he acts and communicates. So, to communicate with your guinea pig and develop a good relationship, you need to understand how these instincts translate into the domestic environment you have created for your pet.

The Wild Life of the Domestic Guinea Pig

To understand guinea pig behavior, you must first realize that guinea pigs are prey animals. In the wild, they live their entire lives constantly on the lookout for larger animals who want to eat them. Each individual guinea pig's ability to be alert, wary, and quick is what keeps him alive.

Wild cavies have a number of behaviors that help them avoid predators. In fact, every behavior guinea pigs possess is designed to help them survive in the wild. The old adage "there's safety in numbers" applies to the wild cavy, who lives in social groups known as herds. Life in a group provides the guinea pig with security on a couple of levels. First, the more guinea pigs there are, the safer it is for each individual animal. For every guinea pig who lives in the colony, there is another set of eyes scouring the landscape, looking out for enemies. When one guinea pig spies a predator, he signals the others that danger is near.

Group Hierarchy

In addition to their instinct for self-protection, guinea pigs also have a set of behaviors that enable them to live peacefully within their community groups. Like many other animals that live in groups with members of their own species, guinea pigs have a complex hierarchy. Each guinea pig herd contains a dominant male and a dominant female, with various other forms of dominance and appeasement in the group. This hierarchy also contributes to the survival of the species, since the stronger, dominant animals are most likely to outlive the lesser members of the herd and go on to reproduce.

Guinea pig burrows provide another form of protection against predators. Since herds construct a network of burrows, there is rarely a shortage of holes to dive into when an enemy approaches.

Understanding Your Guinea Pig

Always remember that guinea pigs are prey animals and are easily frightened. When you sense your guinea pig is afraid, speak to him in a soft voice and move slowly. This will help him distinguish you from an attacking predator, who would move quickly and aggressively.

Your guinea pig may appear to be afraid of something or someone that you consider harmless. Try to put yourself in his position. Since he does not have the power of reasoning that humans do, he is not able to understand why he shouldn't be afraid of something that we know is innocuous. The guinea pig's motto is, "flee first, ask questions later."

Know, too, that your guinea pig's ears are very sensitive because they were designed to be able to detect the subtle sounds of approaching predators. This also makes them sensitive to noises in the human environment. Booming sounds such as loud music, a television, or even shouting can drive a guinea pig to distraction. For this reason, noise should be kept to a minimum. The kindest thing a guinea pig owner can do is to create a quiet, soothing atmosphere for their pet.

Guinea pigs in the wild have a regular feeding schedule that they stick to every day. Given this, the most natural time for your guinea pig to eat is in the

Wild guinea pigs live in colonies and find safety in numbers. Your pet will also get reassurance from the company of his own kind.

morning and evening. Try to provide your pet with breakfast and dinner at the same times every day.

Keep in mind, too, that young guinea pigs differ from older guinea pigs in their behavior and attitudes. Guinea pigs less than 4 months old have not reached maturity. This means they will often behave rambunctiously, much like a puppy or kitten. In the wild, these tendencies would help them learn to cope with life, teaching them to become active in the ways of a guinea pig herd.

Young guinea pigs tend to be particularly active when it comes to chewing and urinating in inappropriate places. Neutering or spaying can help, as can plenty of tolerance and understanding on your part. Patience is key to helping a guinea pig get through this "teenage" period. A more mature and less troublesome adult will undoubtedly emerge.

Body Language

As you spend time with your guinea pig, you will begin to notice that your pet has certain mannerisms and vocalizations that may seem odd. Because guinea pigs communicate with body language and sounds, most of the behaviors you are witnessing are messages about how your guinea pig feels about you and his environment.

The guinea pig's first instinct is always to flee from the unusual and scary.

Playing Dead

Wild cavies lie motionless on their backs to fool predators into thinking they aren't alive. They are playing dead. This posture is designed to squelch the predator's instinct to attack (many predators are attracted by the movements of small animals). If your guinea pig becomes extremely frightened when approached by strangers or other pets, you may see him roll over on his back and lie there without moving. If this happens, reassure him that everything is okay and take him out of the situation that is scaring him.

Stretching

A stretched-out posture is a relaxed one. Your guinea pig will lengthen his body across the floor and rest quietly. It will be obvious that he is comfortable and at ease.

Stiffened Legs

A guinea pig who is prepared to exert his dominance will rise up with his legs stiffened. This stance usually wards off any advances by other guinea pigs, but if the intruder doesn't back off, a fight may ensue.

Nose Touching

Guinea pigs greet one another by touching noses. This is a friendly gesture, usually reserved for familiar acquaintances. You may find your guinea pig offers you this greeting, as well.

Nose touching and nuzzling are friendly greetings.

Jumping

The term *jump for joy* could have been coined by a guinea pig owner, since this is a typical expression of happiness in guinea pigs. Young guinea pigs are known especially for something called *popcorning*, where they leap straight into the air.

Vocalizations

Guinea pigs are vocal creatures, and they like to communicate by sound. The average guinea pig makes a wide array of noises, each meant to communicate something to his herdmates—and to humans.

Squealing

The squeal of a guinea pig is unmistakable. Its high-pitched sound pierces the air. In the wild, cavies use squealing as a warning to let their herdmates know a predator is approaching. It is also a sound for pain and fear and is often a cry for attention. The squeal is also used to beg for food, but only with humans.

Cooing

The sweet sound of a mother guinea pig cooing to her babies is very pleasant. Guinea pigs use this sound to reassure fellow adults, as well. People who have very special relationships with their guinea pigs are also rewarded with cooing sounds.

Gurgling

The gurgling sound of a happy guinea pig is another reward for special humans. Gurgling is an expression of contentment and happiness. If your guinea pig gurgles at you, you can bet you are doing something right!

Teeth Clacking

The sound of chattering teeth means "stay away" in guinea pig language. This is a warning intended for other guinea pigs, nosy pets, and certain humans. Ignoring this sound can result in a nasty bite from an aggressive guinea pig.

If you have two guinea pigs, you can learn a lot about the way they communicate by simply watching them interact.

Chapter 10

Having Fun with Your Guinea Pig

While many people think guinea pigs are boring creatures who just sit in a cage all day doing nothing, those who keep guinea pigs as pets know this is far from true. Guinea pigs have gained an undeserved reputation as uninteresting animals because, until recently, they were primarily kept outdoors where they had little human contact. Today, however, many people keep their guinea pigs inside the house where they can interact with the whole family. Even many outdoor guinea pigs now get to spend some time indoors, roaming through the house and bonding with their humans. Given the guinea pig's newfound opportunity to show us what she's all about, it's not surprising that people are discovering what a unique and fascinating pet she really is.

Time Out of the Cage

Your guinea pig's most basic needs for shelter, food, and water can be met inside her cage, but this is just the bare minimum. Your guinea pig needs exercise, companionship, and mental and physical stimulation. To be a happy, healthy guinea pig, your pet needs regular time out of her cage every day. She needs this time to exercise, explore her environment, and remain stimulated and curious. In addition, you can't enjoy your guinea pig much when she's in her cage. To get to know your guinea pig and let her get to know you and her home, she'll need to be out of her cage. You got your guinea pig in the first place so you could enjoy her as a pet, right? But you just can't turn your guinea pig loose in your home and expect everything to be safe. There are a few things you need to keep in mind:

- If you can't supervise your guinea pig at all times when she's out of her cage, make sure she's in a secure area where other pets can't get to her.
- Make sure the area in which your guinea pig will be playing is guinea pig proof (see chapter 5).
- Be aware of where your guinea pig is at all times. Watch your feet, and be careful shutting doors. Look out for your pet before you put anything on the floor in your guinea pig's space.
- Use the time to get to know your guinea pig better.

Playing

In the wild, guinea pigs are playful creatures who love to engage in games. Like their wild ancestors, pet guinea pigs also like to play. Solitary play is a popular pastime of guinea pigs, who will happily amuse themselves with simple toys. But guinea pigs especially love to play with one another.

The best way to enjoy a guinea pig at play is to give her a toy or let her run loose with a familiar guinea pig companion and then sit back and watch the

Many household items make great toys, including plain paper bags.

Favorite Guinea Pig Toys

Guinea pigs are fun-loving pets who appreciate a variety of playthings. Try offering your guinea pig

- A toilet paper spool
- A small cardboard box
- A paper grocery bag
- A paper cup
- A straw basket

Commercially made toys can be more expensive but just as fun for your guinea pig. Try some colorful plastic tubing that can be fitted together in different shapes or a play gym sized just for guinea pigs.

fun. Guinea pigs love to run around, leap on and off cardboard boxes, chase one another through tubes, and jump over one another. Young guinea pigs also enjoy popcorning—jumping straight up in the air. Two guinea pigs will sometimes play tug-of-war.

There are a number of household items that make excellent toys for guinea pigs. Try offering your pet any of the following objects listed in the box above. Rotate your guinea pig's toys so she doesn't get bored with them.

Traveling with Your Guinea Pig

If you go on a picnic, can you bring your guinea pig with you? What if you are going to visit a relative a couple of hours away? The answer to these questions is, "It depends." It depends on your guinea pig and how you plan to get there. Certain guinea pigs enjoy getting out of the house once in awhile, and if you take proper precautions, you should be able to keep your traveling guinea pig healthy.

Before you travel out of state with your guinea pig, check with the veterinary association for the state in which you'll be traveling. Find out if the state has restrictions pertaining to pet rodents.

By Plane

Airplane rides are not recommended for guinea pigs unless it is absolutely necessary. If you are going on vacation and you need to take a plane, your guinea pig would be better off if you left her at home. The stress of flying will not be good for your guinea pig. If you have to fly with her, book your flight early so you can reserve a space for your pet in the cabin. You will need to purchase a special carrier approved for use inside the cabin of an airplane. You will be expected to keep your guinea pig under the seat in front of you at all times. Be sure to verify with your airline that pet rodents are allowed on board.

By Car

Guinea pigs can ride comfortably in cars on cool days when the traffic is minimal. (They are sensitive to car exhaust.) If you want to find out if your guinea pig is one of these adventurous types who enjoys travel, you'll need to get her used to the idea of riding in the car and being out of her usual surroundings.

Start by leaving her travel carrier in a place where she can have as much access to it as possible. Since guinea pigs feel most secure in small enclosures, you'll find that your pet will actually enjoy spending time in her carrier. Place some hay in the carrier to encourage her to visit it often.

Once your guinea pig seems at ease with the carrier, you can start preparing for outings by taking her for short rides in the car. Make sure you do not take her out on hot days, since guinea pigs are very prone to heatstroke. Wait until the evening for your rides, if possible. Start out by taking twenty-minute drives and then gradually lengthen your trips. If your guinea pig is the traveling type, she will eventually get used to the routine and will settle down and relax.

Once your guinea pig feels okay about riding in the car, you can try taking her on a short trip. Watch her carefully to see if she seems frightened or anxious when you arrive at your destination. If she is, you may want to reconsider traveling with her. If your guinea pig seems comfortable and is enjoying her adventure, you may have a real traveler on your hands. She may be the type of guinea pig you can take with you when you go to visit friends or spend a day picnicking in the park.

Some guinea pigs enjoy getting out and about with their people.

Staying at Home

Since new situations often cause stress and anxiety in guinea pigs, and new environments can mean exposure to disease and parasites, many guinea pig owners decide to leave their pets home when they are traveling. These owners will ask a knowledgeable and responsible friend to take care of the guinea pig, or will hire a professional pet sitter while they are away.

When you are traveling with your guinea pig by car, be sure to take precautions to protect her from the heat. Cover her carrier with a towel to shield out the sun, and use the air conditioner on warm days. Never leave your guinea pig—or any pet for that matter—in a parked car in the heat of the day, even with the windows rolled down. The temperature inside the car can rise quickly and can kill your guinea pig in a matter of minutes.

Remember, too, to bring along some of your guinea pig's necessities. A supply of her regular food is a must, including fresh hay, which should be placed in her carrier for her to munch on. Her water bottle and a jug of the water you usually give her are also necessary. (Providing her with familiar water will ensure that she will drink as much as she needs.) Try to stick to her normal feeding schedule so as not to disrupt your guinea pig's system.

Showing Your Guinea Pig

Some people who start out as pet owners eventually decide to show their guinea pigs. Showing can be a fun activity for the entire family. People who begin by showing a pet cavy often become deeply involved in guinea pigs and end up acquiring a number of animals.

One of the downsides of showing your pet is the pressure it places on her. Showing is stressful for any animal, and guinea pigs are no exception. There is also a greater chance your pet will contract a contagious disease from another guinea pig at a show.

4-H

If you and your family want to investigate the world of guinea pig shows, you may first want to look into 4-H, an organization developed in the early part of the twentieth century to help children learn about how to care for and exhibit livestock. The 4-H youth program has grown to be a large national network of local clubs, featuring projects that range from computers to cattle. Guinea pigs have proven to be a very popular 4-H project over the past several decades. 4-H is an excellent way for young guinea pig owners to learn how to show guinea pigs and care for them.

The mission of 4-H as a whole is to promote farming as a way of life and to help young people develop their potential to learn. 4-H clubs are located around the country and are managed by the nation's land-grant universities. General guidelines have been established by the United States Department of Agriculture (of which 4-H is a part), and individual states follow these rules while establishing their own regulations for clubs in their jurisdictions. The cooperative extension services in each state administers the state's 4-H clubs, which are open to children ages nine to nineteen (and sometimes younger, depending on the individual club).

4-H is a great way to learn about the best way to care for guinea pigs.

Unless you plan to show, it doesn't matter if your guinea pig is a purebred. She's still your snuggly pet.

Typical 4-H guinea pig projects feature hands-on learning in a family environment. Children are taught how to feed, care for, handle, groom, and show their guinea pigs. 4-H clubs are run by volunteers, usually parents whose children have been involved with the program for some time. Individual 4-H projects, such as guinea pig shows, have leaders as well. These people are usually parents and also tend to be breeders or former breeders who have spent a substantial amount of time showing guinea pigs.

Shows specifically for 4-H guinea pig owners are held around the country. These shows follow the rules and breed standards established by the American Rabbit Breeders Association (ARBA), the official organization for guinea pig showing. 4-H members can also exhibit their guinea pigs at county fairs, since 4-H often has a strong presence at these events.

Aside from valuable learning and hands-on experience, members of 4-H guinea pig projects can also earn awards. While the specific awards and requirements vary from club to club, typical activities, such as displaying a winning guinea pig project in the local 4-H fair or successfully exhibiting a guinea pig at a show, can earn participants medals, ribbons, or certificates.

If your child has a guinea pig that is not a purebred, he or she can still show the animal in 4-H under the showmanship class. In showmanship, the exhibi-

ACBA National Specialty

Every year, the American Cavy Breeders Association (ACBA) sponsors a National Specialty show where the finest show guinea pigs from around the country gather to be judged. A regional cavy club is chosen each year to host the show, which is held at a venue in the host club's area. Cavy breeders and exhibitors from around the United States come to the event with their prize cavies in tow.

Cavies are judged at the show in a number of classes, including breed and variety, Best in Show, and Reserve in Show.

In addition to classes, the ACBA specialty features cavy sales and auctions, award presentations, banquets, and raffles, as well as camaraderie for cavy lovers. Breeders and fanciers of purebred guinea pigs have a chance to meet one another and socialize at these fun events.

tor presents the guinea pig to a judge, demonstrating a knowledge of guinea pig care and anatomy as well as proper handling. Children are graded on their ability to present the animal properly and to understand their pet's overall health. The rules for showmanship classes are established by ARBA, which also offers these classes in their regular shows.

To obtain information on a local 4-H guinea pig project, contact your county extension office by looking in your telephone directory. For general information about 4-H, contact the National 4-H Council listed in the appendix.

American Rabbit Breeders Association

ARBA is the governing body for guinea pig showing and registration in the United States. ARBA sanctions guinea pig shows around the country, which are attended by guinea pig fanciers who are very serious about showing. The shows are put on by the American Cavy Breeders Association and its regional guinea pig clubs.

ARBA has a list of rules and regulations for guinea pig shows, and each sanctioned show operates by these rules. Judges who officiate at ARBA shows evaluate purebred guinea pigs using the breed standards published by ARBA. Guinea pigs that are exhibited at ARBA shows may be registered with the organization, but this is not mandatory.

Guinea pigs at ARBA shows are judged in classes organized by breed. Within the breed classification, guinea pigs are then divided by age before they are judged. Awards are given to individual class winners, as well as Best of Breed, Best of Opposite Sex (given to the best guinea pig of the opposite sex of the Best of Breed winner), Best of Variety or Group, and ultimately Best in Show. Class winners usually receive a ribbon; Best of Variety or Group, a rosette; Best of Breed, a trophy; and Best in Show, a larger trophy. Small cash awards are also given to some of the winners.

When competing in ARBA shows, guinea pigs can also earn legs toward their Grand Championship. Three legs qualify a guinea pig as a Grand Champion, which is a distinctive title in the guinea pig world.

Registration

It is not necessary to register your guinea pig in order to show her. However, many people choose to do so since having a registered guinea pig ensures that the animal's pedigree is true and that the guinea pig meets all the requirements of her breed.

Exceptional guinea pigs can become champions.

What Is a Breed Standard?

A breed standard is a detailed description of the perfect guinea pig of that breed. Breeders use the standard as a guide in their breeding programs, and judges use it to evaluate the guinea pigs in shows. The standard is written by ARBA.

The standard includes a description of every part of the guinea pig, from her coat to her size to her ears, eyes, and nose. It lists the general faults for each breed and all general disqualifications from competition. It also includes a detailed description of each color and pattern recognized within each breed.

To register a guinea pig in the purebred classification, the animal needs a three-generation pedigree. The guinea pig must be examined by an official ARBA registrar, who will determine if the guinea pig is eligible for registration. The guinea pig must be 6 months or older and weigh thirty-two ounces or more. She must also be free from disqualifications or eliminations, as defined by the breed standard.

To register a guinea pig, you, as the guinea pig's owner, must be a member of ARBA. You will also have to pay a fee for registering your animal.

Registrars are present at ARBA-sanctioned shows. To have your guinea pig registered, you must bring the guinea pig and her papers to the show, or make arrangements with a registrar to inspect the guinea pig at the registrar's home. It takes about three weeks to receive your registration papers in the mail, once the examination process is complete.

Ear Tags

If you go to a guinea pig show, you will notice that many guinea pigs have a small metal tag in one ear. You may also see an ARBA registrar putting ear tags on guinea pigs right there at the show.

For a guinea pig to be shown at an ARBA show, she must have a metal tag with an identifying number attached to her right ear. When a guinea pig is registered with ARBA, the registrar places the guinea pig's registration number on a

The lovely show guinea pig on the left has an ear tag for identification.

tag and then attaches the tag to the ear at the time of examination. Many breeders do their own tagging, using a system of letters and numbers they have created for their record-keeping purposes.

Some people decide not to show their pets since they do not wish to tag their animals. A tag leaves a permanent mark on the guinea pig's ear, and the process causes pain, albeit brief (similar to having your ear pierced), to the guinea pig.

Appendix

Learning More About Your Guinea Pig

Some Good Books

American Rabbit Breeders Association, *Standard of Perfection: 2001 thru 2005*, American Rabbit Breeders Association, 2001.

Brehend, Katrin, *Guinea Pigs: A Complete Pet Owner's Manual*, Barron's, 1991.

Elward, Margaret, and Mette Ruelokke, *Guinea Piglopaedia: A Complete Guide to Guinea Pig Care*, Ringpress Books, 2004.

Gurney, Peter, *Proper Care of Guinea Pigs*, TFH Publications, 1999.

Gurney, Peter, *The Sex Life of Guinea Pigs*, TFH Publications, 2000.

Morales, Edmundo, *The Guinea Pig: Healing, Food and Ritual in the Andes*, University of Arizona Press, 1995.

Sigler, Dale, *A Grown-Up's Guide to Guinea Pigs*, Writer's Showcase Press, 2000.

Vanderlip, Sharon, *The Guinea Pig Handbook*, Barron's, 2003.

Guinea Pig Publications

Critters
Fancy Publications
P.O. Box 6050
Mission Viejo, CA 92690
(949) 855-8822
www.animalnetwork.com/critters

Cavies Magazine
29 Brecon Way
Downley, High Wycombe
Buckinghamshire, UK HP13 5NN
cavies.magazine@ntlworld.com

Popular Pets: Guinea Pigs
Bow Tie, Inc.
P.O. Box 6050
Mission Viejo, CA 92690
www.animalnetwork.com/animalnetwork/small-animal.aspx

Health Resources

House Rabbit Society
1524 Benton St.
Alameda, CA 94501
(510) 521-4631
www.rabbit.org
Provides information on how to find a veterinarian who is experienced in treating rodents. Some regional chapters are involved with guinea pig rescue.

International Veterinary Acupuncture Society
2140 Conestoga Rd.
Chester Springs, PA 19425
www.ivas.org

American Holistic Veterinary Society
2214 Old Emmerton Rd.
Bel Air, MD 21015
(410) 569-0795
www.ahvma.org

GuineaLynx.com
guinealynx.com
Online medical care guide for guinea pigs.

WWWWiz, Vet
wwwiz.com/QandA/animals.html
Common questions about guinea pig health answered by an online vet.

National Cavy Associations

American Cavy Breeders Association
16540 Hogan Ave.
Hastings, MN 55033
www.acbaonline.com
This site includes a list of local and regional guinea pig clubs.

American Rabbit Breeders Association
1925 S. Main St.
Box 426
Bloomington, IL 61704
(309) 827-6623
www.arba.net

National 4-H Council
7100 Connecticut Ave.
Chevy Chase, MD 20815
(301) 961-2800
www.fourhcouncil.edu

Regional Cavy Clubs

Oregon Cavy Breeders Society
34801 Row River Rd.
Cottage Grove, OR 97424
ocbsociety.tripod.com

Golden State Cavy Breeders Association
1360 Sawtooth Dr.
Hollister, CA 95023

San Gabriel Valley Cavy Breeders Association
5862 El Palomino Dr.
Riverside CA 92509
cavy.org/sgvcba/index.html

Grand Canyon State Cavy Club
1157 E. San Angelo Ave.
Gilbert, AZ 85234

The Piggie Pow-Wow
301 Santa Elena SE
Rio Rancho, NM 87124

Sooner State Cavy Club
620 N. 14th
Enid, OK 73701
soonerstatecavy.freeservers.com

The Cavy Ark
194 Greene 619 Rd.
Paragould, AR 72450

Utah Cavy Breeders Association
2037 West Lindsay Dr.
Taylorsville, UT 84119
ucba1st.freeservers.com

Pioneer Cavy Fanciers
6032 Clinton
Boise, ID 83704
webpak.net/~skolstad/pioneer/info.html

C.L.A.S.S.
4502 Rainwood Avenue
Northport, AL 35473
mywebpages.comcast.net/classcavies

Lone Star Cavy Club
1225 Dutch
Deer Park, TX 77536
lonestarcavies.freeservers.com

Texas Cavy Fanciers
408 Fleming Dr.
Hurst, TX 76053
www.texascavyfanciers.com

Columbine Cavy Club
3105 W. 44th Ave.
Denver, CO 80211
home.attbi.com/~columbinecavies/wsb/index.html

Michigan Cavy Breeders Association
12145 Seymour Rd.
Gaines, MI 48436
mcbacavy.homestead.com

Ontario Cavy Club
295 Oakdale Ct.
P. O. Box 1506
Corunna, Ontario N0N 1G0 Canada
ontariocavyclub.com

River Valley Cavy Fanciers
153 County Rd. JJ
River Fall, WI 54022

Hoosier Cavy Fanciers
418 E. Jefferson St.
Tipton, IN 46072
members.tripod.com/~HoosierCavyFanciers/index.html

Ohio Cavy Club
2377 Route 54
Urbana, OH 43078-9215

New York State Cavy Fanciers
2748 Lakes Corners Rd.
Clyde, NY 14433
angelfire.com/ny3/nyscf

Mid-Atlantic Cavy Breeders Association
826 Anderson St.
Trenton, NJ 08611
cavy.osb-land.com/macba

North Carolina Cavy Breeders Association
228 Packs Rd.
Glenville, NC 28736
www.getciw.com/nccavy

On the Web

Cavy Information

www.landfield.com/faqs/pets/guinea-pig-faq
Most frequently asked questions about guinea pigs answered

www.oinkernet.com
Tons of links to guinea pig sites all over the world

www.guinea-pigs-guinea-pigs.com
General guinea pig information

www.buddies.org/kvhome.html
Miscellaneous information on guinea pigs

www.guineapigs-online.com
Guinea pig information page

Product Catalogs

Care-A-Lot Pet Supply Warehouse
www.carealotpets.com

Cherrybrook
www.cherrybrook.com

Doctors Foster and Smith
www.drsfostersmith.com

Pet Warehouse
www.pets-warehouse.com

Summit Pet Products
www.summitpet.com

Index

Photo credits

Tammy Raabe Rao/Rubicat Design & Photography: title page, 8–9, 10, 11, 13, 14, 15, 16, 18, 19, 21, 23, 24, 26, 32–33, 34, 35, 37, 38, 39, 40, 43, 44, 45, 46, 49, 50, 52, 56, 57, 58, 59, 60, 62, 63, 66, 68, 69, 72, 73, 75, 77, 78, 80, 82, 83, 84, 85, 86, 89, 91, 92, 94, 95, 96, 98–99, 100, 102, 103, 104, 105, 106, 107, 109, 111, 112, 114, 116

American Rabbit Breeders Association: 27, 28, 29, 30

Kathy Anderson: 53

Printed in the USA
CPSIA information can be obtained
at www.ICGtesting.com
JSHW012011140824
68134JS00023B/2364